Advance Comments on
Getting Straight A's

"This is a splendid book . . . a very insightful and eminently practical guide. It should be most helpful to undergraduate and graduate students and all those who want to discipline their minds and grow intellectually."

—Terrel H. Bell
Professor, The University of Utah and
Former Secretary of Education

"At last—a lucid study guide that provides sound advice and is fun to read. Gordon Green may just be the new 'Dale Carnegie' on how to succeed in school!"

—Sar Levitan
Author, Research Professor, and
Director, Center for Social Policy Studies
The George Washington University

"Thoughtfully conceived, clearly written, and right on the mark! Gordon Green's book will show you how to become a straight-A student, while at the same time making school a memorable experience rather than a grind."

—Sheldon Haber
Professor of Economics
The George Washington University

"Parents: If you want your children to succeed in college, then make sure they read GETTING STRAIGHT A'S. It will increase the quality of your own life!"

—Dr. Murray Weitzman
Economist, statistician, and a
parent who has seen these study
methods work for his own children.

Getting Straight A's

Getting Straight A's

by Gordon W. Green, Jr., Ph.D.

Lyle Stuart Inc.   Secaucus, New Jersey

Published by Lyle Stuart Inc.
120 Enterprise Ave., Secaucus, N.J. 07094
Published simultaneously in Canada by
Musson Book Company,
A division of General Publishing Co. Limited
Don Mills, Ontario

Address queries regarding rights and permissions
to Lyle Stuart Inc., 120 Enterprise Ave.,
Secaucus, N.J. 07094

Manufactured in the United States of America

20 19 18 17 16

Library of Congress Cataloging in Publication Data

Green, Gordon W.
    Getting straight A's.

    Bibliography: p.
    1. Study, Method of.   2. Examinations—Study guides
3. Report writing.   I. Title.
LB1049.G729   1985   371.3'028'12   85-8005
ISBN 0-8184-0380-2

For my three children,

HEIDI, DANA, and CHRISTOPHER

*in order to make their future lives
a little easier and much fuller*

ACKNOWLEDGMENTS

Several individuals played key roles in the development of this book. First and foremost, I would like to thank Harold Roth, my literary agent, who believed in me from the outset and provided expert advice on how to improve the book. I was introduced to Harold by my good friend Ben Wattenberg, who supplied encouragement and tutoring throughout the endeavor. Kathy Italiano, my secretary, tirelessly and cheerfully typed several versions of the manuscript during her off-duty hours. Dr. Murray Weitzman and two of his children, Gary and Paula, were among the first to show that my study methods could be generalized to others. Professor Sheldon Haber, of The George Washington University, read the manuscript and made many helpful suggestions. There were many other professors, too numerous to mention, who provided the instruction that helped form the basis for this book. And last, but by no means least, I wish to thank my dear wife, Maureen, who absolved me of my household duties and offered the encouragement needed to bring this work to fruition.

A moment's insight is sometimes
worth a life's experience.
　　—Oliver Wendell Holmes
　　　　The Professor at the Breakfast Table

FOREWORD

If it has always been your wish to get "straight A's" in school, and you are willing to do a reasonable amount of work to achieve that goal, then this book is for you. It is designed for persons taking undergraduate as well as graduate courses in college. It is based on a unique system of study that I developed while attending graduate courses in economics in the evening and working full time during the day at my regular job.

I am confident that the system will work for almost anyone, because I never came close to getting straight A's in college before I developed it. After putting the system to work as a graduate student, I was able to get an A on every test in every course I took. Moreover, I had plenty of time left over for leisure activities. The secret was that I knew exactly what was required to get an A in a course. Other students who have applied my methods have also become straight-A students.

The methods presented here are applicable to practically any discipline in college and will accommodate almost any personal lifestyle. This book has something important to offer you, whether you are attending college as an undergraduate or a graduate, full- or part-time, or a high school student getting ready to enter college. Considering the high correlation between success in college and later life, it may be one of the most important books you ever read!

Gordon W. Green, Jr., Ph.D.

CONTENTS

12

PART FOUR

MAKING THE SYSTEM WORK FOR YOU

PART ONE

Reflections on Education

1
INTRODUCTION

How many times have you brought your grade report home at the end of a school term, only to get the following reaction from your parents?

"Why can't you do better in school? I told you that you were going to have to pay a stiff price for all of the time you goofed-off during the semester. It kills me to think of how you're wasting our hard-earned money. At this rate, you'll be lucky to stay in school, and luckier still to find a decent job if you graduate. When I was in school . . ."

And so it goes. Does this sound familiar? Probably more familiar than you care to admit. I know that I have certainly heard it more times than I care to remember.

One thing we all have in common is that we have been pressured to do well in school from our earliest years. Your parents told you that you needed good grades to get into college and that very good grades were required to get into the "right" college. And if you are already in college, you no doubt feel the pressure to get high grades. The pressure may come from your parents, who want to be convinced that they spent their money wisely; or, if you are no longer accountable to your parents, it may come from your own self-awareness that good grades not only give you a great deal of personal satisfaction, but are often a requirement to get the "right" job after graduation.

Another thing we all have in common is that we want to do better. Whether you are currently a mediocre student or an average or good student, you know that you could and should be doing better. As Robert Browning, the English poet, once wrote, "Ah, but a man's reach should exceed his grasp, or what's a heaven for?"

Despite the general recognition of the importance of getting good grades, very few people have performed at the highest levels. A whole continuum of achievement is apparent in the average classroom, ranging from students who seem to be totally lost, to one or a few students who stand head and shoulders above their peers. It is similar to the ancient concept of the "Great Chain of Being," in which everything is carefully ordered from lowest to highest in rank. Except in this case, the apex is not presided over by God. It is held by the students who seem always to have the correct answers to the teacher's questions, and who earn an A on practically every test. I previously regarded these elite few as geniuses who were capable of something I would never be able to accomplish.

The conventional wisdom that only geniuses and bookworms are capable of getting straight A's in school is definitely incorrect. Geniuses are often bored with the mundane material presented in the classroom. For example, Albert Einstein performed poorly in school before going on to extend human knowledge well beyond its previous frontier. And bookworms are compulsive readers who often lack the discipline to score high on structured examinations.

If not geniuses and bookworms, then who does make straight A's in school? Very few people, indeed, but more are certainly capable of attaining this elusive goal. You, in particular, are capable! Regardless of where you are presently located on the "Great Chain of Grades," you have the potential to perform at the highest level and make straight A's. It goes without saying that those with a high degree of innate intelligence will find the task easier, but even those with average intelligence are capable of reaching the top. Most people have not become top-notch students either because they did not know how to go about it or they thought the cost was so high that it was not worthwhile.

What is required for success? The first prerequisite is to recognize that no matter how difficult this task may seem, you are capable of achieving it. Marcus Aurelius, the Roman Emperor, recognized the importance of this frame of mind almost 2,000 years ago when he said, "Do not think that what is hard for thee to master is impossible for man; but if a thing is possible and proper to man, deem it attainable by thee." This attitude worked a long time ago and it still works today.

How do I know that it still works today? I know from my own experiences, and the experiences of others who have used my methods, that it is possible to become a straight-A student—regardless of past performance. During various stages of my lifetime, I have been a mediocre student, as well as an average and outstanding student.

My grades were so poor in high school that I almost did not get into college. I had to go through a special trial program in order to be admitted into a state university which prided itself in opening the doors of education to all residents. Once in the university, I fumbled and struggled with the rest of the students, and almost did not survive the first year.

In his epic *Paradise Lost*, John Milton wrote, "Long is the way and hard, that out of hell leads up to light." Well, long and hard it was, but I finally saw the light.

I was a better than average student during my last two years as an undergraduate and an outstanding student in graduate school. I earned my Ph.D in economics by taking two graduate courses a semester in the evening, while often working more than 40 hours a week at my full-time job. With such a busy schedule, and family responsibilities as well, I realized that I needed some type of system to keep from going under. The system I developed not only kept me on top of things, it enabled me to make an A in every course I took! In fact, I made an A on every test in every course I took! My system was so foolproof that, even with a busy schedule, I had plenty of time left over for leisure activities.

Now I know what you must be thinking. An A on every test in graduate school after almost not getting into college? Dr. Green must be one of those weird eccentrics. Just because it worked for him does not mean it will work for me. All I can say to that attitude is what Napoleon Bonaparte once told one of his generals, "You write to me that it's impossible; the word is not French."

In the next chapter, I will document how other students have become straight-A students by using my methods—students who had average or erratic experiences before adopting my methods. What did we have in common? We knew exactly what was required to make an A in a course and we were willing to do the necessary work to achieve it. We also had that important ingredient that Marcus Aurelius spoke of—we knew that our goals were attainable.

Well, what is this system that I keep referring to and how does it differ from what other educators have to say? Let's look first at what others have to say.

There are any number of study guides available on the market, some issued very recently. These guides claim to increase your proficiency in any number of study skills: how to read a book, how to take a test, how to become a better student, and so forth. They offer a broad range of information on study skills, but do not show you how to put it all together in any systematic way to become a straight-A student.

Who writes these books? The authors typically come from a rather narrow range of occupations, such as guidance counselors, psychologists, and psychometricians (persons who design tests). Their study methods are usually based on the experiences of groups of students observed under laboratory-type conditions. They tell you what works best for different types of students under different conditions. While this information is useful, in my mind it is not a good substitute for the experiences of someone who has actually become a top-notch student.

I have an even more serious problem with some of these study guides. They overwhelm the student with a mass of information on study tips and lay out a schedule of activities that even a Tibetan monk would not be willing to follow. They are typically very broad in scope, attempting to teach you everything from what you should have learned in grammar school to how to pass the Graduate Record Exam. Some would have you fill out an endless number of charts, diagrams, and calendars to allocate and monitor practically every hour during the entire semester. In short, they violate a fundamental principle stated by Confucius aeons ago, "To go beyond is as wrong as to fall short." A more serious deficiency, in my opinion, is that some of these guides provide just plain wrong advice, as I will describe later.

What is my system about? Well, if you are a good reader, I probably do not even have to tell you. You would have known to review the table of contents, chapter headings, and chapter summaries before lunging into the book. This not only gives you a general idea of what the book is about, it provides a framework to help organize the information as you read. I will be teaching you the fundamental skills needed to become a successful student, such as how to read a book, how to take a test, and how to write a term paper.

The heart of the book is Part Three, on "A System for Getting Straight A's." In.it I have distilled everything I know from years of education to show you how to most effectively understand the material presented in lectures, get the most from your studies, prepare for exams, and receive A's on exams. Part Four provides additional insights and study tips that will enable you to maintain success for the duration of your educational training.

What is my philosophy for success? Why, it's as old as philosophy itself. It is the wisdom of the ages.

It is what Plato meant when he said, "The absolute natures or kinds are known severally by the absolute idea of knowledge."

It is what Aesop meant when he said, "Put your shoulder to the wheel."

And it is what Virgil meant when he said, "These success encourages: they can because they think they can."

That's right. The wisdom of the ages. If you know what you are doing, work hard, and have confidence that you will succeed, then you will succeed.

Over 2,500 years ago, the Chinese sage Lao Tzu said, "A journey of a thousand miles must begin with a single step." You have taken that step by opening this book. The rest of the journey will be up to you.

PRINCIPLE 1
You can become a straight-A student if you know what you are doing, work hard, and have confidence of success.

2
SUCCESS STORIES

Everyone loves success stories. Why? Because if others have succeeded then it is entirely possible for us to as well. We are particularly fond of stories in which someone has turned the situation around and succeeded against the odds. We are impressed not only by their accomplishments, but by the realization that our success may not be as difficult as we first thought. Our attitude becomes one of, "If they can do it, then I can do it too!" That's not a bad attitude to have, because it indicates that you are starting to believe in yourself—one of the key ingredients for success.

Included in this chapter are three case histories that clearly show how students have been able to raise their performance in school to the highest levels by using my methods. The case histories include my own educational experiences as well as the experiences of two other individuals who recently used my methods in undergraduate courses. They illustrate that these methods work for undergraduate and graduate students, full-time as well as part-time students, persons studying different disciplines, and persons with a limited amount of time to devote to their studies. We all became straight-A students by using the methods presented here, even though we had experienced difficulties earlier in our educational careers.

I am going to provide a very detailed description of my own experiences. I do this because, like Henry David Thoreau, "I should not talk so much about myself if there were anybody else whom I knew as well."

There is a more serious reason why I provide such a detailed account of my experiences. My description is very much a review of my mistakes and, as you will soon see, I have made more than my share compared to most people. I do not delude myself into thinking that you will be able to avoid all of the same mistakes, just because you have heard about them beforehand from me. But I will consider my efforts a success if you can avoid just a few of the mistakes I have made—particularly if you avoid the most detrimental ones!

First of all, I make the disclaimer right at the outset that I am neither a genius nor a bookworm. I have not always found education to be easy and I do not enjoy having my face buried in a book all of the time. There are too many other interesting and challenging things to do. I am a firm believer in Francis Bacon's pronouncement that, "To spend too much time in studies is sloth."

Unfortunately for me, when I was in high school in the early 1960s my attitude was that "*any* time spent in studies is sloth." I paid little attention to my studies and preoccupied myself instead with the other things I found enjoyable. My parents had convinced me that going to college was in my own self-interest, but I had very little discipline to prepare myself for the task. Consequently, my grades in high school were marginal and teachers labelled me as an underachiever. Some of the teachers said I was "college material" and they tried to convince me to be more serious about my studies. Other teachers, including one guidance counselor, felt that I was a lost cause and tried to discourage me from even applying for college.

It was not until my senior year that I began to devote some attention to my studies, but by then it was a little late and much more difficult since I had missed much of the foundation material presented earlier. I made mostly D's—and even several F's—in my junior level courses, and I was only able to raise my grade-point average slightly during my senior year. Even though I was working harder, I found school to be quite a struggle. I was enrolled in the academic program, but my grades were so poor that I received only a general diploma upon graduation from high school.

The real shock came when I applied for college. Alfred, Lord Tennyson, once wrote in a poem, "Too late, Too late! Ye cannot enter now." That's the same response I got from several colleges when I applied for admission, albeit in more modern English.

The University of Maryland finally agreed to give me a chance, mainly because they are required to consider all applicants who are state residents. Because of my poor high school grades, I had to enter a special pre-college program for students who did not meet the basic entrance requirements. The program, which consisted of courses in English and social studies, was an intensive program designed to weed out students who were really not college material.

In his play *King Richard II*, Shakespeare referred to, "The caterpillars of the commonwealth, which I have sworn to weed and pluck away." Well, we were the caterpillars that the University was trying to weed out of its commonwealth, and only about half of us survived the harvest. It was at this point that I realized how difficult the course ahead of me was going to be.

Upon entering the University, I tried to strengthen my reading and comprehension skills by attending a special reading laboratory. This helped me to overcome some of my basic shortcomings from improper preparation as a high school student, but still left me far short of what was required to do well in college. However, the program at least provided me with the basic skills needed to survive the rigors ahead.

As with many students who first enter college, I was not sure of the field to select as a major. I started off with a major in general business administration, but later changed to economics. Although economics has often been referred to as "the dismal science," I found the subject enjoyable because I could relate the classroom material to what was happening in the "real world."

Even though I sincerely wanted to do well in college, my first two years were a near disaster. Besides not having the proper preparation for college, I did not have even a basic understanding of how to study or prepare for a test. Moreover, even if I had possessed the understanding, I did not have the discipline to do the work. Living in the college dormitory, with all of its associated distractions, did not help the situation. As a result, my grades were very poor and I came very close to not making it through. I received several D's in my courses during the first semester.

I was not alone. Many of my classmates were in the same predicament. Many of the current generation of students are in the same predicament. In fact, many students down through the ages have been in the same predicament; they have made the same mistakes over and over again. They are guilty of what Sir Thomas Browne, the English author, called "an old and gray-headed error."

The source of the error is that students do not study continuously throughout the semester. They follow the philosophy of Matthew Browne, "Never do today what you can put off till tomorrow." This is not a bad philosophy *per se*, as long as the things that are postponed can wait until tomorrow. The problem is that everything gets put off until tomorrow, even if it needs to be done today. Studies are often given a lower priority than the seemingly endless variety of diversions available to college-age students, such as sporting events, parties, dating, and other non-academic affairs.

I can remember procrastinating in my studies until just two or three days before an exam, and then I would panic. By studying very intensely, I would try to ram into my head in two or three days time all of the information presented since the last exam. This usually required a hasty review of all the reading materials, at least the parts I had highlighted with a magic marker. It also required several reviews of my haphazardly constructed class notes, which always convinced me that I never fully understood the material in the first place. And if I became really anxious, I would try to utilize every minute available before the test by cramming all night—commonly known as "pulling an all-nighter." The objective was not to learn the material, but merely to make it through the test with a passing grade.

The body and mind do not take kindly to this kind of forced-feeding. Spending a couple of days cramming for an exam or "pulling an all-nighter" creates anxiety, dilutes one's self-confidence, and prevents the mind from properly organizing the material. If one has taken drugs to stay awake during the whole ordeal, these problems are only magnified. The student goes into the exam in a dazed state, often remembering only the last bit of material reviewed. Students in such a state cannot think clearly about the questions, and often try to force their responses into the material they have remembered by rote. The usual result is failure to answer the exam questions in a satisfactory manner. The whole experience is like a bad dream that reaches a climax on the day of the test, lingers until you receive your grade, and then recurs as the next exam approaches.

Does that study routine sound a little familiar? Probably more familiar than you care to admit. Well, rejoice! After you read this book you will not have to go through it again.

It is a miserable way to go through school. The only consolation for students who go through such an ordeal is the companionship of others in the same situation. I can remember the conversations I used to have with some of my fellow students who were in the same situation. We would complain about the difficulty of exams, or that we only scored high enough to get by with a passing grade. We would commiserate with each other about the difficulty of our situation and start to feel that the faculty was conspiring against us. We always felt that our problems were the fault of someone or something else: the teacher was trying to trick us, the test was too difficult or unfair, if only I was asked about the material I know, and so on. We never considered that we ourselves might be the source of the problem.

For many students in such a rut, what could have been a very enjoyable experience is turned into a nightmare. Benjamin Disraeli, the great English statesman, once said, "A university should be a place of light, of liberty, and of learning." During my first two years in college, it felt more like a torture chamber. I can vividly remember being afraid to take an exam because I did not know the material. I can also remember the feelings of guilt when my grade was returned, because I had not studied enough to do well on the exam.

Many students cannot hold up under this pressure. The drop-out rate during the first few years of college is very high. Many of my friends dropped out because they felt the whole experience was a hassle, and they longed to get out into the working world where they could make some money. I was determined to stick it out and graduate. During my second year I was only able to raise my grades to mostly C's, with an occasional B here and there. I still did not have any confidence in myself and I would often do very poorly on tests and in courses.

Upon reaching my third year in college, my study habits began to improve and so did my grades. I had at least learned to take better notes in class, and to start studying for an exam before the eleventh-hour. I was taking more courses in my major (economics), so I was building on previously acquired knowledge. I raised my average to a solid B, and even made an occasional A in courses. Although I did not realize it at the time, I was actually developing study methods that I would later build into a complete system. Since I had not yet perfected my system, I was struggling with my studies and had to work very hard.

My last two years in college were just the opposite of the first two years. I violated that fundamental principle stated by Confucius, "To go beyond is as wrong as to fall short." I was working so hard on my studies that I did not have the time I needed for leisure activities. And my life was dull—dreadfully dull. That's what happens when you spend all of your time on studies. Although I was doing better scholastically, I also longed to get out of school, get a job, and start making some money, because the whole experience seemed like a hassle. I definitely was not ready for graduate school.

After graduation, I took my first permanent job working as

an entry-level statistician for the U.S. Government. What a shocker! I went from the delusions of grandeur one experiences as a student in economics to the reality of being a clerk working in a "bullpen" full of other clerks. The transition from the academic to the working world is particularly difficult for economics students. The student works with models of the entire economy, and analyzes changes in important policy variables. As a clerk working for the government, my only job was to verify numbers that should have been checked by the computer in the first place. And I was suffering from mental anguish and boredom.

Many people beginning their first job experience the kind of disenchantment I have just described. There is the obvious difficulty of adjusting to the change from attending a few hours of classes a day to sitting at a desk all day, as is commonplace in most professional jobs. But the more fundamental difficulty is that many of the interesting jobs are not immediately available. It usually takes a considerable amount of job search or achievement within a given organization to find one's niche, and some people never do. As Thomas Carlyle, the Scottish historian, once said, "Blessed is he who has found his work; let him ask no other blessedness."

I was determined to find "my work." After floating around in the government for a few years, I finally settled into a job I enjoyed at the Census Bureau. The job involved the preparation and analysis of statistics on income distribution and poverty. I began to think back about the courses I had taken as an undergraduate and how enjoyable they really were. Moreover, I began to see the possibilities of applying some of the things I had learned in school to my actual work experience. This is what makes work challenging.

It was at this point that I decided to return to college. But before going on to graduate school in economics, which was my ultimate aim, I realized that I needed to ground myself firmly in mathematics and statistics. These fields are very important for students of economics, because the discipline is heavily quantitative. As an undergraduate, I had taken only enough mathematics and statistics to graduate, and these were the courses known as the "cake" or "cookbook" courses—just enough to meet the basic requirements to graduate.

I enrolled in mathematics and statistics courses at the University of Maryland evening school, while continuing to work full time at my regular government job. It was during the period of taking these courses in the evening and working during the day that I developed my system of study. As I will describe in Part Three, I developed a complete system of what to study for an exam, when to study it, and how much to study to ensure an A in a course. I was able to make an A in every mathematics and statistics course that I took at night school. I was very proud of my accomplishments, because I was taking the more difficult theoretical courses designed for mathematics and physics majors. Before this, I had failed high school trigonometry and made only marginal grades in my undergraduate mathematics courses designed for non-mathematics majors.

This was an important turning point for me. I had managed to confront and master the subject which I feared the most—mathematics.

After finishing my courses at Maryland University, I enrolled in the Ph.D. program in economics at The George Washington University. I took two graduate courses each semester, while continuing to work full-time at my regular job. By this time, I had perfected my system almost to a science. I kept using the same principles that I had developed in night school all through graduate school in economics, and they worked in every course I took. They even worked in non-economics courses that I took as electives. Not only did I receive an A on every test in every course I took, I had plenty of time to burn. Extra time was something I needed direly, because the combination of working at a demanding job, attending school, and taking care of home and family made for a a very busy schedule indeed. I was finally able to enjoy what Cicero called, "leisure with dignity." I began to think how easy it would have been if only I had known these principles as an undergraduate.

My system enabled me to get a Ph.D. in economics. The

topic I chose for my dissertation was the examination of earnings differentials between men and women, and Blacks and Whites, who recently entered the labor market. There was a lot of interest in my dissertation and it received national attention. It was described on the front page of *The New York Times* (January 16, 1984), appeared in other newspapers across the country and in *Fortune* magazine, and I was interviewed on CBS Morning News to discuss the findings. Many people were amazed at the amount of news coverage devoted to a Ph.D. dissertation. I attribute all of this good fortune to my system—without the system, none of it would have been possible.

I have gone through a rather elaborate discussion of my own personal experiences because I think that my case illustrates the power of my system. If a student who almost was not admitted into college because of poor grades is able to get a Ph.D., and receive straight A's in the process, then the system should work for almost anyone. But you are entitled to some hard evidence that my system can actually be generalized to work for others.

A couple of years ago, I told a close friend, and former colleague, about the system of study I used to get straight A's in graduate school. Dr. Murray Weitzman told me that his son Gary was an undergraduate student in college and asked if I would explain my system to him.

After talking to Gary, I realized that there were many striking similarities between our background and experiences. Gary is a very outgoing young man who has many interests in addition to his studies. His performance in high school was only average and he described himself as a "mid-C student." He started off as a general business student at the University of Maryland and later changed his major to economics. During his first two years in college Gary had received mostly C's and some B's in his college courses. More importantly, he felt that he was not getting as much as he should out of his college experience.

It was late in the Spring semester of 1982 when I spoke to Gary, so there was not enough time to put the system to work that semester. During the Fall semester of 1982, Gary started using my system selectively in his major courses, and noticed that his mastery of the material was increasing. Although his grades did not improve markedly that semester, Gary started to realize the power of my system.

Gary was at a significant turning point. He could either put my system into effect or stay with his old study methods. He decided to use my system on all of his courses in the future.

Here is the difference that it made. During the Spring of 1983, Gary was taking a full load of courses in economics, government and politics, and American studies. He used my system on all of his courses and made all B's and A's. In the courses in which he received a B, he was right on the borderline of making an A. This success gave him a lot of encouragement and he was determined to use my system even more vigorously the next semester.

Francis Bacon once wrote, "Knowledge is power." Well, here is an example of the power a knowledge of my system will bring. In the Fall of 1983, Gary was again taking a full load of courses in economics, sociology, education, and human development. He applied my system in all of his courses and he received straight A's. This was a tremendous accomplishment considering his past experiences. He applied my system in his next and final semester and missed receiving an A by only a few points in one of his courses. Gary told me that he let up a little in that last semester, as many do, because he was anxious to graduate and move on to something new.

There are some other factors that need to be taken into account in assessing Gary's accomplishment. During the semester in which he made straight A's, Gary was living at home and working about 20 hours a week at a job while taking a full load of courses. Moreover, the improvement in his grades enabled him to get a job as a teaching assistant in an advanced undergraduate labor-management relations course. Even with his busy schedule, Gary found that he had plenty of time to pursue leisure activities such as basketball and golf.

Another aspect of Gary's accomplishment is even more noteworthy. Gary recently told me that my system builds a lot of self-discipline and confidence and changes one's outlook about attending college. He began to look forward to attending class and participating in the learning experience. He found that when he spoke up in class it was more often to answer a question than to ask one. The whole experience became more enjoyable and his friends noticed a definite change in his behavior and accomplishments. He stands in sharp contrast to the multitude of students who go through college and receive little more than the "sheepskin." His accomplishments in school will enable him to continue his education with graduate studies or get a job in a good line of work.

Dr. Weitzman also told his daughter, Paula, about the system of study that I had explained to Gary in the Spring of 1982. Paula Weitzman Borsos graduated from high school in June 1975. Although Paula had been an above-average student in high school, with a "low-B" average, she did not have confidence that she would do well in college. She had not devoted much time or effort to her high school studies and, like many of us, was suffering from "math anxiety." As a result, she did not enter college immediately upon graduation, but decided instead to spend one year in Israel and then worked for one year in a bank.

Paula had very sporadic episodes in college over the next several years, because she could not decide whether she really wanted to be in college. She entered the University of Maryland in the Fall of 1977, but dropped out of school after one semester to work in a bank. Paula returned to the University in the Fall of 1978 as an economics major, but again dropped out to go back to work, this time for almost a full year. Not satisfied with her experience in the working world, she returned to Maryland University in the Spring of 1980, spent two consecutive semesters as a marketing major, one semester as a textile major, and then finally dropped out of school again because she was dissatisfied with the whole experience.

Paula's experiences during this period are similar to those of many students in college. They do not really want to be in college and they do not know what field to select as a major. They are hoping to find a sense of direction and purpose in their efforts. But while most of these students stay in college continuously and suffer, Paula had the courage to follow her heart and drop out of college when she did not really want to be there.

As with many students in a similar situation, Paula's grades went downward during this sporadic period. She did very well in her first semester because her fear of school and lack of self-confidence led her to spend almost all of her waking hours on her studies. During her second and third semesters as an economics and marketing major, she was able to maintain a low-B average. By the time she switched to a textile major in the Spring of 1981, her grade point average had dropped to a C. Her studies were clearly on a downward spiralling path.

During the next two years, Paula did not attend school, but instead moved to New Jersey, worked for several firms, and got married. Dr. Weitzman explained my system of study to Paula in the Spring of 1982, during her visit back home to see her family. She knew of Gary's success in college using my system, and she was anxious to try it herself. Paula and her husband relocated in the Washington, D.C., area in the Spring of 1983, and she decided to try her hand at college again, this time more determined than ever.

When Paula re-entered the University of Maryland in the Fall of 1983 she was a changed person, and her experience since then has been an unqualified success. She is now majoring in accounting, and in her first semester back at school she took a full load of courses in accounting, statistics, and other electives. By using the methods presented here, she earned all A's and B's in her courses that semester. In the Spring of 1984, Paula again took a full load of courses in accounting, finance, and economics. She applied my methods even more vigorously in that semester and earned straight A's in all of her courses. Paula is now a very serious and competent student in her senior year who is determined to do well in her studies. Unlike her past experience, she now enjoys going to school and looks forward to attending classes.

Well, are you now convinced that you can become a straight-A student? These three case histories clearly show that even students who have experienced difficulties in their studies can become straight-A students. If you are an average—or even below-average—student, then you are capable of accomplishing the same. If you are an above-average student, then the task should be even easier. Henry David Thoreau summed it up when he said, "I know of no more encouraging fact than the unquestionable ability of man to elevate his life by a conscious endeavor."

PRINCIPLE 2

If others who have experienced difficulty in school have become straight-A students, then you are capable of the same.

3

THE IMPORTANCE OF YOUR EDUCATION

C. A. Helvetius, the 18th-century French philosopher, once said, "Education makes us what we are." In a very real sense, education does make us what we are. We are very much the product of what we have learned and experienced in the past. Your education determines your knowledge about a particular subject, affects your value system and beliefs, and influences your way of looking at almost every facet of life. Most importantly, your education has an influence on the type of occupation you will hold in our society and on the general level of well-being you and your family will enjoy.

Almost anyone you talk to will acknowledge the importance of a good education. As stated by Publilius Syrus, the Roman philosopher, "It is only the ignorant who despise education." Persons at the lower end of the economic spectrum embrace the conventional wisdom that their life would have been so much better if only they had continued their education. Parents in this class push their children to study hard and further their education so they will have more opportunities in life. And given the high correlation between education and income, persons at the upper end of the economic spectrum are usually the first to emphasize the importance of a good education.

Although some individuals acquire great wealth by inheritance or sheer luck, most will acknowledge that their education played a key role in opening the doors to success. They are likely to emphasize the importance of education for obtaining a job that is personally rewarding both psychologically and financially, and for expanding one's capacity to enjoy the experiences of life.

I think it can be fairly stated that the two major benefits of a high-quality education are increased wealth and personal enjoyment. Let's explore these ideas more closely.

The capacity to enjoy and appreciate life is enhanced by a fuller understanding and mastery of its mechanisms. The range of possible experiences and intricacies of life are so great that we can never know them all. The so-called "liberal education" attempts to acquaint the student with as many different subjects as possible.

Our early years of education provide the broadest possible opportunity for learning about the world. It is a time when Shakespeare's saying, "Why, then the world's mine oyster, which I with sword will open," is most relevant. We progress through the elementary and secondary educational systems almost as true generalists, studying subjects ranging from the purely esoteric to the totally practical. Mastery of a broad range of information is very important for developing complete individuals, people who are more comfortable with the world in which they live and have a better understanding of what makes it go around.

Unfortunately, the oyster gets opened only part way. We retain only a small amount of the material presented in school, as parents who help their children with homework will readily confirm. (A saving grace is that many of the parents master the material during the second or third time around as they assist their children.) Much of the material is missed in the early years because students do not have good study habits, and most never develop good habits.

In college, we also have an opportunity to take a wide range of courses, particularly during the first two years. This enables us to build up a huge storehouse of knowledge in the form of facts, principles, and theories. This knowledge also helps us to gain a much fuller understanding and appreciation of the world in which we live.

There is an opportunity to use this understanding almost every day of our lives. For example, a knowledge of chemistry and physics helps us to better understand the make-up and behavior of our physical world; a knowledge of botany helps us to see more in a flower than its radiant beauty; a knowledge of geology provides new meaning to a visit to the Grand Canyon; a knowledge of zoology increases the enjoyment of going to the zoo, and the list can be extended indefinitely. Acquisition of such knowledge turns commonplace encounters into interesting experiences, and helps us to see and understand the world in its enormous vibrancy, complexity, and splendor.

An even more important aspect of the knowledge obtained in college is the ability to see and understand the interrelationships between various facts, principles, and theories.

Henry James, the great American novelist, once wrote, "Really, universally, relations stop nowhere, and the exquisite problem of the artist is eternally but to draw, by a geometry of his own, the circle within which they shall happily *appear* to do so."

In the truest sense, James is correct that "relations stop nowhere," but a college education at least enables us to "draw a circle" around the major interrelationships between various facts, principles, and theories. You will find that you can better relate what you have learned in one course to your knowledge in other courses, as well as to everyday experiences. For example, your understanding of history will be enhanced by your knowledge of economics and government and politics. Even routine activities such as reading the daily newspaper take on added significance. This knowledge gives you a better understanding of the significance of past events, the expectation of future events, and helps you to solve new problems more effectively.

A good education also helps us to develop new interests and

make new acquaintances, making life more interesting and enjoyable. Life would be very boring if we were in a perpetual rut without ever encountering anything new. As Samuel Johnson, the English author, wrote a couple of centuries ago, "The joy of life is variety."

In college, you will take courses and read books in a variety of interesting fields such as literature, art, and music. Knowledge of these areas will provide new sources of enjoyment from reading novels, going to museums, or listening to symphonies. This will broaden your perspective, make you a more complete person, and show you how to enjoy the finer things in life. You will no doubt meet professors and other students with similar interests who will share in this appreciation. In fact, one of the most enjoyable aspects of college is the broad range of people you will meet with different interests, different abilities, and different beliefs.

Contact with a broad range of people helps us to appreciate the extreme degree of diversity in the world. As noted by Michel Montaigne, the French essayist, "There never were in the world two opinions alike, no more than two hairs or two grains. Their most universal quality is diversity." Through education, we come not only to understand and to tolerate these individual differences, but to appreciate them as well.

Attending college also develops more self-confidence and responsibility in individuals because they have greater control over their destiny. With college, you don't have to wait until old age to develop confidence. College helps you to become a more independent thinker because you spend a good deal of your time developing these skills. Whether you are reading a book, attending class, working problems, writing papers, or taking tests, these tasks require you to develop your thinking abilities.

As you become a more able thinker, you begin to realize that you can solve a myriad of problems by yourself. Your self-confidence soars from the realization that you can make your own way without following the advice of others. You become more critical in your thinking rather than accepting everything stated by an "authority." By acting—rather than reacting—in response to developments, you feel that you are part of the process and at least have some control over the outcome. Those who do not have an understanding of developments, or who feel controlled by circumstances, are much more likely to experience alienation. How do you guard against alienation? The philosopher John Locke said, "The only fence against the world is a thorough knowledge of it."

Yes, college can do many things to make you a better person, but one also needs to think about the afterlife—that is, life after college. Considering the amount of time, money, and effort spent on a college education, we should have a clear idea of our objectives. How about you? Do you have a clear idea of your goals? As Plato once said, "The life which is unexamined is not worth living."

You should make a careful assessment of your personal situation and establish your goals while still in college. Ask yourself a few basic questions: What do I hope to accomplish by attending college? Is my primary goal to complete the course work necessary to enter an occupation that is both intellectually and financially rewarding? Am I trying to increase my income and social status and attain a new life-style? Or is my interest the more general one of wanting to become an educated person? Am I there mainly to learn new things, receive intellectual stimulation, increase self-realization, and broaden my personal perspectives?

Your goal may be any one or a combination of the above, or perhaps something I have not mentioned. There is no right answer. (There are wrong answers, however—you don't have any goals, you are just marking time, or you are there only because your parents want you to to be there.) Whatever your goals, establish them firmly in mind so that you can develop behavior to meet your objectives and monitor progress toward that end. You will feel much better about your situation if you can see progress toward your objective.

It may be helpful if you take a few minutes to write your goals on a piece of paper to remind yourself of what you are trying to accomplish. This can be a handy reference when you are distracted from your studies or start asking basic questions like, "What am I doing here?" At these times, you can glance at your goals and you will have an added incentive to work hard. By checking your progress periodically, you can modify your behavior as necessary to accomplish your goals. Since we live in a dynamic world, we have to recognize that our goals themselves may change at different stages of the college career. If your goals have changed, you will need to change your behavior to meet your new objectives.

The most important thing to remember is that goals are not reached immediately; it takes a considerable amount of time and effort to reach them. Being keenly aware of your goals helps you to develop "tunnel-vision" so you can accomplish your objectives in the most timely and efficient manner.

I am certain that everyone has given some thought to the job they will hold after graduation, regardless of their motivation for attending college. As the 17th-century Japanese philosopher Ihara Saikaku keenly observed, "The first consideration for all, throughout life, is the earning of a living."

I am going to devote considerable attention in this chapter to the world of work and income. Considering that I have spent all of my working life studying this subject, it is the area I know best. This should help you to formulate your goals and have some idea of what to expect when you go out into the working world, if you are not already there. I will address several issues, such as what to expect in the way of jobs, what employers are looking for in prospective employees, and how much extra income you can expect to earn from your college education.

Your mission in the working world will be much more specialized than what you have been accustomed to in the academic world. This should come as no surprise, if you have been observant, since specialization starts in college. Although most colleges insist on a broad range of subjects in the first or second year, the student is quickly placed on a track leading to more specialization. Not only do we specialize in a particular subject matter, we specialize in a particular area within a subject matter; in graduate school we specialize even further. The working world requires even more specialization, particularly if we are part of a large organization in which tasks are well defined.

Specialization is essential for efficient production in our highly industrialized and technological economy. This has been going on for a long time. The rapid pace of technological advance in this country will likely lead to even more specialization in the future. With specialization comes mastery of a particular area, which often brings personal satisfaction. By concentrating on a very narrow part of a very narrow field, however, the individual starts to lose touch with the rest of the world. That's when a firm grounding in a general education can provide a good base to lean on.

Current research indicates that the American economy is undergoing fundamental structural changes in the types of jobs created. Whereas manufacturing was the growth leader in past decades, the new leaders are services and high technology. The high-technology jobs tend to have a high concentration of technology-oriented workers, such as engineers, scientists, mathematicians, computer specialists, and so forth. Service jobs include the rapidly growing fast-food industry, and various other personal service jobs. During the past decade, employment increased dramatically in the service and high-technology areas, and declined in manufacturing. These employment trends are expected to continue in the future.

Some analysts have argued that these structural changes will result in higher income inequality in the United States. Many of the service jobs tend to be routine, low paying, and require little in the way of formal education. On the other hand, the high-technology jobs are often more interesting, better paying, and most accessible to persons who have formal training in science and engineering fields. Not only does one start at higher rates of pay in these jobs, there is more opportunity for even higher rates of pay with the accumulation of experience. One's accessibility to the different types of jobs will largely be a function of the quantity and quality of education possessed.

John Ruskin, the English author, once asked a very telling question, "Which of us . . . is to do the hard and dirty work for the rest—and for what pay? Who is to do the pleasant and clean work, and for what pay?" Do you think it will depend on a person's education? Do I really have to answer that question for you?

Competition for the better jobs has been fierce in past years, and will likely continue in coming years. There was keen competition for jobs in the past decade, as millions of workers of the baby-boom generation entered the workforce. The baby boom consists of the more than 75 million persons born during the two decades after World War II. These persons have entered the labor force in record numbers, as evidenced by the fact that the total labor force has grown by more than 30 million persons since the beginning of the last decade. Although many of the members of this group had high levels of education, the abundance of workers resulted in some occupational mismatch since not everyone could enter their chosen field. The sheer volume of job entrants with a college degree lowered the earning power of a college degree. These developments resulted in a lot of frustration for the younger generation. Competition for the better jobs will continue as the last of the baby boomers enter the labor force during this decade.

Enrollment rates in college have increased for the present generation as well, particularly for women. In fact, there are now more women enrolled in college than men, and more are entering the disciplines traditionally studied by men. According to the latest statistics from the Census Bureau, there are more than 12 million persons enrolled in college and more than half are female. Women in college today are much more likely to major in fields traditionally studied by men, such as science and business and management. As the members of the present generation enter the workforce in the coming years, the better jobs will go to the better qualified.

With all of these highly educated persons coming into the labor force, do you think employers will be choosy? Do you think a person's grades will be important? Do I really have to answer that question for you, either?

As a supervisor who has hired many workers, I personally know the importance of good grades in the selection process. During the past decade, I have reviewed hundreds of applications for a few available jobs. Since it was impossible to review every application in detail, I instructed our personnel office to restrict the applications to individuals whose grades were mostly in the A to B range. This reduced the number of applications to a manageable workload, which I could pursue further with personal interviews, review of past work, and so forth. I found that many of my fellow supervisors were using the same approach in screening job applicants.

Why would employers do this? After all, we were running the risk of overlooking some very competent and qualified workers who did not score well in college, for whatever reason. Why did we do it? Simply because our expectation was that those who had done the best in college were likely to do the best in the workplace. Aristotle summed it up over 2,000 years ago when he said, "Educated men are as much superior to uneducated men as the living are to the dead."

An employer faced with hiring an unfamiliar person to fill a job vacancy is a classic case of economic uncertainty. The employer does not know the actual productivity of the applicant, so he looks for other characteristics that are expected to correlate with productivity. Education provides an important signal to the employer in this regard. Education is only a signal, however, because a high level of education does not necessarily guarantee a high level of productivity. In fact, many people argue that education does not increase productivity at all, since we do not acquire skills that are directly applicable in the marketplace.

The individual who has completed a college degree, however, is likely to be someone who will stick with a task and see it through to completion in a job setting. As the philosopher Herbert Spencer once said, "Education has for its object the formation of character." In addition, a person who has scored well in college is likely to be regarded as someone who is mentally sharp and trainable. The importance of being trainable cannot be overemphasized, since practically all jobs require a certain extent of training. Therefore, a person who has completed college and done well in the process is likely to have a significant advantage over his peers when competing for jobs.

How much is your college degree worth in terms of actual dollars and cents? After all, there is nothing wrong with thinking about increasing your income. According to the English novelist Jane Austen, "A large income is the best recipe for happiness I ever heard of. It certainly may secure all the myrtle and turkey part of it."

We can obtain a better idea of the extra earning power of a college degree by examining some recent statistics from the Census Bureau. Benjamin Disraeli once remarked, "There are three kinds of lies: lies, damned lies, and statistics." Well, here are some statistics that do not lie.

A college education will definitely secure more myrtle and turkey for you. Based on a 1984 survey, of men working year-round, full-time, those with four or more years of college had average annual earnings of $30,990, about 48 percent higher than the average annual earnings of high school graduates ($20,870). The comparable comparison for women working year-round, full-time indicates that those with a college degree received earnings ($18,580) that were, on average, about 39 percent higher than high school graduates ($13,410).

The earnings difference between men and women with similar levels of education is a function of many factors, such as differences in field of study, differences in occupational distribution, differences in the length and continuity of lifetime work experience, and so forth. There is evidence that women are starting to enter the type of jobs traditionally dominated by men in the past, such as accounting and professional and technical jobs. As women enter the types of jobs traditionally held by men, and stay in the workforce for a longer period of time, the earnings gap between the sexes should narrow in the future.

The difference in earnings between high school and college graduates is magnified when considered over one's entire working life (up to 65 years old). Do you know why? Persons with a college degree are more likely to enter skilled occupations that will yield even greater rewards later on in their career. Earnings continue to increase sharply over most of the working life in professional-level jobs, whereas earnings tend to flatten out or even decline in later years in non-professional jobs. As Aristotle said long ago, "Education is the best provision for old age."

How much of a difference does education make over a lifetime? As an approximation, let's make the conservative assumption that earnings increase at about the same pace as inflation, so "real earnings" stay about the same. In this case, males working year-round, full-time who are college graduates would earn about $1.9 million over their lifetime compared with $1.4 million for male high school graduates. The comparable figures for women working year-round, full-time are $1.2 million for college graduates and about $870,000 for high school graduates. Since earnings should increase faster than prices in the future, there should be more real income for everyone. But one thing is for certain —the earnings gap between high school and college graduates will always be there. We like to think that these large income differences are justified because college graduates are more productive in the labor market than high school graduates.

This simple mathematical exercise with lifetime earnings clearly demonstrates the importance of a college degree to your financial well-being. Furthermore, it should be noted that the figures cited are only averages for the group. There is a substantial dispersion of earnings levels around these group averages. Good achievement in college may help put you on the upper side of the average rather than the lower side. If you obtain more than four years of college, you can expect your earnings to be even higher.

Although luck sometimes plays a role in the fortunes men reap, the predominant influence on your economic well-being will be your own behavior. We usually get what we deserve.

You are the master of your own destiny. But in order to reach that destiny you must know what your goals are and work to achieve them. As suggested by Epictetus, the ancient Greek philosopher, "First say to yourself what you would be; and then do what you have to do." In the final analysis, it's all up to you.

PRINCIPLE 3
Carefully formulate your goals and develop behavior to accomplish those goals.

SUMMARY

PART ONE
REFLECTIONS ON EDUCATION

PRINCIPLE 1
*You can become a straight-A
student if you know what you are
doing, work hard, and have
confidence of success.*

PRINCIPLE 2
*If others who have experienced
difficulty in school have become
straight-A students, then you are
capable of the same.*

PRINCIPLE 3
*Carefully formulate your goals and
develop behavior to accomplish
those goals.*

PART TWO

Learning the Basic Skills

OVERVIEW OF THE
BASIC SKILLS

In his *Essays*, Francis Bacon advised, "Reading maketh a full man; conference a ready man; and writing an exact man."

These are the basic skills that you must master to become a top-notch student. You must be able to comprehend and retain information from reading assignments, understand the theories, principles, and facts presented by your instructor in class, and demonstrate your mastery of the material in a written form, such as in exams, term papers, and other assignments. This section of the book includes three chapters designed to help you master these basic skills: HOW TO READ A BOOK, HOW TO TAKE A TEST, and HOW TO WRITE A TERM PAPER.

Is all of this really necessary? After all, you have spent at least twelve years learning the basic skills to prepare yourself for college. You have no doubt read countless books, taken innumerable tests, and written more compositions and term papers than you care to remember. Surely you must have developed a lot of expertise from all of this experience.

Well, it may all sound very simple, but as Henry Adams, the American historian, once said, "Simplicity is the most deceitful mistress that ever betrayed man."

There is much more to mastering these basic skills than first meets the eye. Do not assume that you will fully understand a book by reading it from cover to cover; or make an A on an examination by carefully working from the first through the last question; or write an innovative and polished term paper by reading extensively and summarizing your notes. No, that won't do it; there is much more involved!

In this section, I will describe the approaches I have developed over the years to help you master these skills. I will show you the steps to become a more active reader, enabling you fully to understand reading assignments from books and articles. I will show you the strategies for making the highest scores on various types of exams, including essay exams, objective tests, problem tests, take home exams, oral exams, and comprehensive exams. And I will show you how to write a comprehensive and innovative term paper that will be enjoyable to write and interesting to read.

Part Three will show you how to use these basic skills in an integrated system to become a straight-A student.

1
HOW TO READ A BOOK

Over 1,500 years ago, St. Augustine implored his countrymen, "Take up, read! Take up, read!" His message is just as pertinent today as it was in the past.

Books contain the knowledge of mankind accumulated over the ages. As Thomas Carlyle observed, "All that mankind has done, thought, gained or been: it is lying as in magic preservation in the pages of books." Books provide us with the opportunity to meet with great thinkers on a one-to-one basis, even if they are of a different locale or time.

More to the point, the books and articles you read in your courses will help you to master the subject matter and score high on exams. Since instructors often develop their lectures from assigned books, a thorough knowledge of the reading assignments will increase your mastery of the material presented in the classroom. And since instructors typically are unable to cover all of the course material in their lectures, the reading assignments will supplement your knowledge about the content of the course.

Over the years, researchers have proposed a number of different reading systems designed to increase comprehension and retention of the written word. This work dates back to 1946, when Francis Robinson wrote *Effective Study*, in which he proposed the SQ3R method (Survey, Question, Read, Review, and Recite). In 1954, Thomas Staton wrote a book titled *How to Study*, which proposed a slightly different method called the PQRST (Preview, Question, Read, State, and Test). Of more recent vintage (1972) is a book written by Mortimer Adler and Charles Van Doren titled *How to Read a Book*.

In general, the various reading systems propose different methods of reviewing summary information, such as that in boldface type, summary paragraphs, topic sentences, and so forth, before actually reading a book or article. The difference is that they disagree on the proper order of these reviews. There is no consensus on which of these systems is best, so I am not going to review them here. (I have listed them in my References if you wish to read further.) What I plan to do, instead, is to describe the method I have found most useful over the years for reading books and articles.

Let's assume that you have just picked up a new textbook assigned for one of your courses. How should you proceed to read it?

The first rule for effective reading is to pick a spot where you can read in comfort. I prefer to wear loose clothing and sit in a big easy chair where I can relax. Don't get too relaxed, however, because you will be less efficient in your studying. Research has shown that slight muscular tension increases efficiency and mental acuity. Reading while sitting at a desk provides just the right amount of tension for some people. You will have to experiment to see what works best for you.

Your reading spot should be relatively quiet and out of the way from major traffic to reduce distractions. Almost all households have a certain level of noise and you should not allow this to distract you. Some individuals can maintain their level of concentration while reading regardless of the level of noise. If you are not one of those individuals, which I am not, then I have a suggestion for you. I like to play a low level of background music on the stereo or radio, which serves the dual purpose of helping me to relax while screening out other distracting noises in the house.

Make sure that your reading spot has ample light so you will not tire unnecessarily or damage your eyes. All too often you will see students reading in a dark corner. Research has shown that your eyes are much less likely to tire under indirect light, such as from a fluorescent lamp, than under direct light. Make sure that the light shines evenly on the page from overhead or behind, so it will not shine in your eyes.

Now that we have finished with preliminaries, how do you go about reading that new book?

It is a good idea to get an overview of the book before lunging into the first chapter. First take a quick look at the title page and read the complete title to get an overall idea of what the book is about. The next step is to read the short statement about the author's background and experiences (usually at the back of the book) to gain some perspective on where the author is coming from. Following this, read the preface or introduction to find out why the author wrote the book and how it is organized. Next, take a look at the table of contents to get a better idea of the overall structure of the book and specific content.

By this time, you have a good idea of what the book is about. If you are reviewing books to determine their relevancy to a topic you are researching for a term paper, you probably know enough at this point to decide whether to continue. Since we have assumed that the book is assigned for a course, let's continue.

Are you ready to start reading the first chapter? It's still too soon. You should obtain an overview of the chapter before reading it—in other words, "look at the forest before inspecting the trees."

Quickly scan through the first chapter to get an overall idea of its structure and content. Read the introductory paragraphs, summary paragraphs, major headings, minor headings, conclusions, and so on. Look at the graphs, pictures, or equations presented in the chapter. This preview helps you to develop a framework to organize the material as you read, facilitating your comprehension and retention of the material. Although you may not realize it, you have just transmitted a lot of information to your mind on a subconscious level. Your mind will be working with this material and communicating with the conscious level as you read, increasing your grasp of the material. Every chapter should be previewed in this way before commencing with the detailed reading.

Although we are discussing the reading of a hypothetical textbook for a course, there are a few points that need to be made about previewing other materials. You should use the same principles presented here for previewing journal articles and other assignments. It should be obvious that you would not want to preview a novel or mystery in the same way. The purpose of these works is to build suspense and preserve the mystery for as long as possible. Reading the middle or back of a book would spoil the plot, just as seeing the ending of a movie before the beginning would ruin it for you.

Okay, you are finally ready to read the first chapter in the textbook. You are probably wondering, "Do I just sit down and read it, or is there something more?" Yes, there is more—much more!

You should try to read the book in an active rather than a passive manner. Active readers not only comprehend more than passive readers, they find the whole experience more interesting and enjoyable. As Henry David Thoreau once said, probably referring to passive readers, "It is not all books that are as dull as their readers." Do you know whether you are an active or passive reader? Let's find out.

A passive reader goes through the motions of reading words without concentrating on what is being read. There is no attempt to understand the author's message, the interrelationships between the ideas, or their relevancy to one's own experiences. Passive readers find themselves drifting off to thoughts of what they are going to do later in the evening, chores that need to be done, how much they miss a loved one, or any number of things they would rather be doing than reading a book. Is it any wonder that they find reading to be dull? They are just wasting their time, because passive reading will not increase their understanding of the course.

How is the active reader different from the passive reader?

The active reader will follow Thoreau's advice in his classic work *Walden*, that "Books must be read as deliberately and reservedly as they are written." The active reader will read the book in a very deliberate manner, sorting out the information presented and understanding the interrelationships between the various ideas. Understanding is not the same as brute memorization, since it is quite possible to memorize without understanding. To understand what you have read implies that you can explain it in your own words and still preserve the author's intended meaning.

The active reader reaches this level of understanding by curiously asking several questions and trying to answer them. He will ask questions such as: What is the book about? What does it say in detail? How does the information fit in with what my instructor has said in class? The active reader also tries to relate the material to his or her own knowledge and experiences. Does the book relate something similar to what I have experienced? Does this new information alter my current knowledge, behavior, or view of the world in some fundamental way? Relating the material to your own experiences makes it more meaningful and easier to retain.

The astute active reader also reads critically, thereby becoming a more creative reader. Reading critically means that you constantly question what the author is saying. Critical questions are of the following type: What questions is the author trying to answer and how does he or she go about answering them? What are the author's assumptions and what is the basis for making them? Are the author's statements based on knowledge, facts, experiences, or opinions? Is the author objective or does his or her work reflect a definite bias? Do you agree or disagree with what the author is saying, and what is the basis for your assessment? If you disagree, is it because the author has not offered evidence for the assertions, or is the logic flawed? You may not know the answers to all of these questions, but by attempting to answer them you have gone a long way toward becoming an active reader.

The questioning process does not end after you have finished the chapter. You should reflect back on what you have read and quiz yourself to see if you have mastered the material before moving on to the next chapter. Make an assessment of what you have learned from reading the chapter.

In addition to the questioning process, there are several other traits of the active reader. They all revolve around the desire to fully comprehend and master everything of significance presented in the book.

In order to grasp fully the author's message you must read and understand all of the words he uses. When you come across words you do not understand, take the time to look them up in the dictionary. Although you can sometimes understand the meaning of a word by its use within the context of a sentence, this is not the best way to master the word. When you look up a word in the dictionary, take a few minutes to study the various parts of the description. Look at the origin of words, how to spell and pronounce them, parts of speech, single and multiple meanings, and so forth. It is especially important to understand the meaning of technical words used in scientific disciplines; if you do not fully understand the technical term then you will not fully understand the principle being discussed.

Looking up words in the dictionary will not only help you to understand fully the author's message, it will expand your vocabulary as well. You will find that you have a better command over words and are able to express yourself more clearly when writing answers to essay questions, not just in English class but in all of your classes.

To understand fully the author's message you should read everything presented. That's right—including the charts, graphs, and tables. Many students skip over these graphical aids, implicitly assuming that the material is superfluous and was placed in the textbook to take up space. You should recognize that this material was presented by the author for a very good reason, and you may be missing something crucial if you skip over it. Sometimes it is possible to see and remember a relationship from a chart, graph, or table in a way that is not readily apparent from the English language.

You should recognize that even if you have read everything

presented, the author's intended message occasionally may not be clearly discernible. Sometimes the ideas and principles discussed in your readings will be very complex, and you will have to dig deeper to understand fully their meaning. As Albert Einstein once wrote in an autobiographical note, "Something deeply hidden had to be behind things."

If this is the case, you may have to re-read the material in a different way in order to fully grasp the content. One approach is to read the material more slowly by concentrating on one sentence at a time. As William Walker wrote in his work *The Art of Reading*, "Learn to read slow: all other graces, Will follow in their proper places." After you read a sentence, pause, and ask yourself what that sentence means before moving on to the next sentence. Try to relate the new idea to what the author has already covered. If you still cannot fully understand the idea, mark the page and skip over it temporarily. After you have read further you can refer back to this passage and there is a good chance that it will be more intelligible. Being able to view ideas within the context of other ideas often helps to solve the mystery, just as we can more fully understand the meaning of words by viewing them within the context of other words in a sentence.

What is the hallmark of the active reader? The active reader uses all of his faculties and senses to master the material. Different persons use different senses for mastering information. Some find that they can learn best through their sense of vision, others are more effective with their sense of hearing, and still others find that physical movement works best. For example, some students find that reading in a silent manner works fine, others find that rehearsing out loud increases comprehension, and still others find that writing something down is the only way to master it. Some like to use a pencil or magic marker as they read, underlining key words, marking main ideas, writing questions in the margins, and so forth. In reality, we use some combination of all of these senses in learning new material. Use the combination that works best for you.

You will know that you are becoming a more active reader when you are able to anticipate the author's next thought or statement before reading it. This indicates that you have discerned the author's purpose and have aligned your thoughts with his.

I would be remiss if I did not say at least something about increasing reading speed in a chapter on "How to Read a Book." Everyone wants to read a book faster because time is a scarce resource and there are plenty of competing activities—including the reading of other books. However, you should never emphasize speed to the exclusion of everything else.

There has been more nonsense written about speed reading than quack cures for cancer. Forget about the advertisements that promise you will be able to read the Old Testament of the Bible in three hours by running your finger down the pages in a zig-zag fashion. That may be the way to locate an entry in the telephone book, but it should be obvious that you will not be an active reader at those speeds. Most of the people who emphasize speed are more interested in turning pages so they can tell their friends how many books they have read, rather than comprehending what they have read.

Let's take a look at the processes involved in reading rapidly. The key to rapid reading is the number of words you can see and understand as your eyes move across the page. Persons who can see a full word at a time can read more rapidly than those who have to read a single letter at a time. And persons who can see several words in a phrase at a glance will naturally read faster than those who can see only one word at a time. Our eyes move across the page in several stops—called fixations—and the more words we can see before stopping, the faster we read.

An additional value of looking up words in the dictionary should now be very clear. If your vocabulary is limited you will not be able to read at a rapid and smooth rate. Every time you encounter an unfamiliar word you must stop abruptly as you try to discern the meaning of the word. Although looking up words in the dictionary takes more time in the short run, your reading speed will increase in the long run because you will be able to read with fewer interruptions.

You will undoubtedly find that you can read different works at different rates of speed, depending upon their complexity. As Francis Bacon once remarked, "Some books are to be tasted, others to be swallowed, and some few to be chewed and digested." Often a novel can be read very quickly and smoothly because you can digest the material as fast as you can read it. On the other hand, many technical writings are highly complex, abstract, and condensed, so you may need to ponder over a statement for some time to understand its meaning. I can remember spending several minutes studying portions of pages in my graduate economics textbooks because of the extreme complexity of the material. Fortunately, reading assignments tend to be less extensive in highly technical courses.

As you gain more experience in reading, you will develop a facility for reading faster. However, you should always make an effort to read all of the words in a passage rather than skipping over them; otherwise, you may not fully understand the author's message. Never force yourself to read at a faster rate than you can handle, or you will find the experience to be very unpleasant. This can lead to anxiety or cause your eyes to tire unnecessarily. Rather than consciously worrying about reading speed, I would encourage you to adjust your reading speed naturally to the rate which allows you to comfortably grasp the material.

You should now have a good idea of the qualities that make an active reader. By becoming an active reader, you can turn what used to be a humdrum chore into an exciting new adventure. The active reader is like an explorer venturing into unchartered areas in search of knowledge and enrichment. If you enter this adventure with an open and enthusiastic mind, you will find the search to be both interesting and exciting. There is a certain satisfaction that comes from finishing a book and making its wisdom part of your own.

If you have not been an active reader up to this point, you should quickly preview the whole book and read the remaining material using the principles discussed in this chapter. Remember . . .

PRINCIPLE 1

An active reader previews a book before reading it, and continually asks the questions that lead to a full understanding of the author's message.

2

HOW TO TAKE A TEST

Charles Colton, the 19th-century English author, wrote in his work *Lacon* that, "Examinations are formidable even to the best prepared, for the greatest fool may ask more than the wisest man can answer." Despite the accuracy of this statement, we must recognize that testing is one of the "facts of life."

Broadly considered, we are tested on practically everything we do. The smallest infant is tested to see when he can talk or walk. The adolescent is tested to see how well he can master the material presented in grade school or show accomplishment on the athletic field. Adults who work are judged by their supervisors on how well they have completed an assigned project. Even nonworking adults are judged by their family on everyday activities, such as preparing a meal. Yes, in the broadest sense, testing is one of those facts of life that begins in the cradle and follows us to the grave.

In a more narrow sense, testing is a very important fact of life that will determine how well you do in college, and what opportunities will be available later on. You are required to take several tests in every course you take, including a lengthy final at the end of the semester. Like it or not, tests are a turnstile that you must pass through to get to the next course, to earn your degree, to be admitted to graduate school, and possibly even to get a job in the working world.

Despite the widespread prevalence of tests, most students are not very test-wise. The ability to take tests and score high is an acquired skill, not an innate ability. Without a knowledge of these skills, the most intelligent and prepared student may do poorly on an exam. As René Descartes, the great French mathematician, once said, "It is not enough to have a good mind. The main thing is to use it well."

In this chapter, I will discuss the basic procedures you will need to follow to become a test-wise student. We will assume, for the moment, that you have done the necessary preparation to make an A on the test. The steps that will enable you to reach this level of preparation are the subject of Part Three, "A System for Getting Straight A's." Although this approach may seem as though I am "putting the cart before the horse," it is possible to examine the basic test-taking skills in isolation. When we get to Part Three, you will know how to use those skills even more effectively to become a straight-A student.

I will discuss the different approaches that should be used for taking different types of exams. This review will cover the basic types of exams given in class, such as essay exams, objective exams (such as multiple choice, true-false), problem exams (in mathematics and sciences), and open-book exams (which allow the use of supplemental materials). I will also discuss the approaches to be used in take-home exams, comprehensive exams, and oral exams. I will not cover the methods used for other exams, such as IQ tests, aptitude tests, and various standardized exams. The reader interested in these types of examinations is referred to a book by Bernard Feder, *The Complete Guide to Taking Tests,* listed in my References.

Before turning to the methods used for each type of exam, I will review a few basic principles that you should follow before taking any exam.

Basic Principles Before the Test

Never arrive late. Always arrive to take your test well before it is scheduled to begin. Avoid hurrying or arriving late because it is disconcerting, you may lose your composure, and you may lose valuable time needed to complete the test.

Bring plenty of supplies. Always be sure to bring plenty of supplies with you, such as pencils, erasers, paper, exam booklets, and any special equipment you will need, such as rulers, calculators, compasses, and so forth. It is unsettling to have to rely on your classmates to supply you with equipment. Would you show up on the tennis court without a racket? Of course not. Be prepared in the classroom as well.

Don't listen to the pre-exam chatter of your classmates. If you arrive early to take your exam, you will hear your classmates testing each other on various topics or making their best guess as to the probable exam questions. Don't listen to it. It is too late to add anything to your knowledge and this chatter will only confuse or disarm you. If it is bothering you, take a little walk outside the classroom to relax and loosen-up.

Read and listen to the instructions. This one is so important that I will say it again, "Read and listen to the instructions." Make sure that you know exactly what is expected of you instead of lunging immediately into answering the questions. Listen carefully to verbal instructions and pay particular attention to the written general instructions on the exam paper. The instructions will tell you which questions you have to answer, the type of answer your instructor expects, the order in which the questions should be answered, and the number of points assigned to each question. All too often students will lunge into answering the questions, only to find out that they have answered the wrong questions. It's hard enough to make an A on a test even if you answer the right questions.

Write your name on the exam paper. If you don't do this, the teacher may give your A to someone else.

These principles are so basic that I am sure you have heard them at least a thousand times. And yet, some have probably been violated in every test ever given. Engrave these principles in your mind.

Essay Exams

In courses other than science and mathematics, essay exams are overwhelmingly the most popular form of exam given in college. As I think back over my college career, the vast majority of the exams given at the undergraduate level were essay in nature and almost all of the exams at the graduate level were essays. Problem tests, which I will discuss later, are the predominant form of test in the fields of science and mathematics. Because of the overwhelming importance of essay exams, I will devote a considerable amount of attention to them.

Why are essay exams so popular with your professors? It is because essay exams not only measure your ability to recall information, but make you demonstrate your ability to analyze, interpret, and apply it in an organized and logical manner. In essence, they test skills that cannot be examined with the ordinary objective exam. Essay exams reveal the reasoning behind answers, and, hence, the students's real understanding of the subject. They are supposed to encourage creativity and the organization of ideas. And they measure the student's ability to express these ideas in a thoughtful and well-written essay—the hallmark of the scholar. As John Sheffield, Duke of Buckingham, once wrote, "Of all those arts in which the wise excel, Nature's chief masterpiece is writing well."

Well, how does one go about writing the good answer to an essay question? Do you just think up the answer and write it down? Far from it—that will only get you into trouble! In order to illustrate the mechanics of taking an essay exam, let's go through each of the steps from beginning to end for a hypothetical exam.

You have just been handed an essay exam in one of your courses. You have carefully read and listened to the instructions and know exactly what you are supposed to do. What do you do next?

The way you spend the first five minutes or so on an essay exam is crucial. Your decisions in the opening minutes will determine which questions you answer, how well you answer them, and ultimately the grade you receive. You have to be very careful or you may get on a wrong track and never recover. A good analogy is running a sprint at a track meet. You have to get off the starting block properly or you will have little chance of winning.

Use the first five minutes or so to look over the exam very carefully. Notice how many questions and pages are in the exam (don't forget the last page). You should read *all* of the questions very carefully before writing an answer to any one of them. You do not want to lunge directly into writing an answer to a question.

As you read through the first question, ask yourself what is being requested. Is the teacher looking for a command over trivia, an understanding of ideas and their interrelationships, an application of basic principles, or what? Read each word of the question, underlining key words that tell you what you are supposed to do. Does the question instruct you to discuss or describe something, to compare or contrast, to develop or demonstrate? These instructions may sound quite similar, but their meaning is distinctly different. A list of key words often used in essay questions can be found in the appendix. You should read them carefully at some point.

If you do not understand every aspect of the question, immediately ask the instructor for a clarification. You will find most instructors to be very receptive to such inquiries.

As you read the first question, write down words or thoughts that come to mind as part of the answer. Make these notes in the margin of your test paper. You need not write complete sentences—a few words will remind you of the thought when you return to the question later to answer it.

All right. You now understand exactly what is being requested in the first question. Do you answer it now? No, not yet. You should read through all of the other questions in the exam using the same approach employed for the first question.

There are three good reasons why you should read all of the questions before attempting to answer any one of them. First, it is desirable to read through all of the questions to find out what will be required of you. Second, the essay questions are sometimes related to each other. Third, and most important, by reading through all of the questions at the outset, you have submitted information to your mind on a subconscious level. Your mind will be working with this information throughout the entire exam, increasing the likelihood that you will come up with a good answer when you eventually get to a particular question.

Let's assume that you have now finished reading all of the questions. If you have a choice, you will need to decide which questions you will answer. As you read each question and jotted down thoughts, you were scanning your repertoire of knowledge about that topic. By this time, you should have a clear idea of the questions you are most comfortable with or knowledgeable about. Common sense dictates that you select these. Don't select a question that you are not very knowledgeable about, just because you are looking for a challenge. You will have plenty of time for challenges when you get out into the working world.

Once you have made your choice, quickly tally up the point score for the questions. You should allow yourself a proportional amount of time for each question depending upon its point score. For example, if you are taking a two-hour test with one 50-point question and two 25-point questions, then you should allow yourself one hour for the first question and a half-hour for each of the other two questions. Make a note of the time you should be starting the second question, the third question, and so forth. Try to stick to this schedule to allow yourself enough time to finish all of the questions. It does not do any good to give a masterful answer to one of the questions and flop on the other two.

Okay, you are now ready to answer your first question. But which one do you answer first? If the teacher has not specified an order, it is wise to answer the easier questions first and return to the more difficult questions later on. Why? If you worked on the difficult questions first, you might become anxious because you are not making any progress and the clock is ticking. If you return to the difficult questions later on, your confidence will be higher and you can deal with them in a more rational manner. This confidence comes from the feeling that you have completed most of the test in a satisfactory manner. Moreover, by working on the difficult questions last, your mind will have had additional time to consider the problem on a subconscious level.

As you return to the easier questions, all that you currently have to work with are the few thoughts jotted down from the first reading. You obviously need more before you can actually start writing the answer. What process should you go through to develop a complete answer to the question? Let's take a few pointers from the philosopher John Dewey, who wrote about the processes of rational thinking in his book *How We Think*.

According to Dewey, there are several different stages in thinking rationally. The first stage is to recognize the problem. What in particular is the instructor requesting on the exam question? Well, you have already decided that from your first reading of the question.

The next stage is to analyze the problem. This means to review all of your knowledge on the subject, break it down into its component parts, and recognize the interrelationships between the parts. You have already done some of this from your first reading of the question. Now is the time to complete your analysis.

The next stage is to generate possible solutions to the problem. After you have analyzed the exam question, you may come up with several different answers that all seem plausible.

The final stage is to test and verify the accuracy and completeness of the possible solutions. In this step, you compare the possible solutions against the question asked to determine which constitutes the best answer. In this last stage, you are throwing out the possible solutions which do not provide a complete answer to the question.

As you go through the various steps in Dewey's process, you will come up with additional information to include in your answer. Write down these points in the margin of your test paper alongside the points you jotted down from your first reading of the question. Again, use words or short phrases to express the thoughts, not complete sentences. By now, you have written down the major points for all of the information that will go into your answer. The next step is to indicate the order in which you will write the information in your answer. This is similar to writing an outline, but you do not have time to do that. Number the points in the order you will write them in your answer.

You are now ready to start writing your essay. Before we discuss how to do that, let's analyze what we have done. I have taken several pages to describe your thought processes in answering essay questions because I have broken these processes down into their component parts. In reality, your mind will go through these steps much more quickly than it has taken you to read these pages. As an analogy, I could have taken several pages to describe how to hit a backhand shot in tennis, but if you know what you are doing it will take only a few seconds to make the swing.

Now, how do you write your essay? Do you just write down the points in the order in which you have numbered them? That's basically it, but let's see if we can impose a little more structure.

Aristotle once said, "A whole is that which has beginning, middle, and end." That is exactly what your essay will require if it is to be a complete response. State the thesis or theme of your essay very clearly in the introduction. Then develop this thesis in the body of the essay. Each paragraph should present arguments, evidence, or reasons to support your thesis. Be sure to mention major facts and ideas as well as examples and supporting details. This illustrates that you not only have general knowledge but in-depth knowledge as well. In fact, mentioning exceptions to the point demonstrates the extent of your knowledge about a point. Also, use the appropriate technical terms to demonstrate that you have a high degree of mastery over the material. And, of course, teachers are impressed by profound statements, particularly if they recognize in them some of the wisdom they have imparted in class. Finally, your essay should have a conclusion which summarizes the thesis.

There is a basic principle that students invariably violate on an essay exam: Answer the question that is asked. Many students write an answer to the question they would *like* to answer rather than the question being asked. Make sure that your response addresses *only* the question asked. Never pad your answer with extraneous information, just in order to have a long response. This will lead the teacher to think you are trying to fake it because you do not know the real answer to the question. It is better to use the principle of "Ockham's razor," stated by William of Ockham, which is, "A plurality must not be asserted without necessity." Remember, you will be graded on how well you answer the question at hand, not on the basis of the extent of your general knowledge!

If it now appears very easy to answer essay questions, remember what Aesop said: "Appearances often are deceiving." Sometimes you will encounter difficult situations in essay exams. Let's examine a few.

Even if you have prepared adequately for an exam, you may encounter a question that you don't immediately know how to answer. When this happens, you have to accept the question as a challenge. If you are not able to arrive at an acceptable answer right away, keep working at it. Attack the problem from a different direction or perspective to try and get a foothold so you can reason through to the answer. Base your answer on hard evidence and avoid using hunches on what you think the answer might be. If the question seems too long and complex, break it up into manageable parts you can deal with. Whatever you do, don't give up. There is a correct answer to the question and you will find it if you are sufficiently persistent and innovative.

Sometimes, no matter how hard you try, you are just unable to come up with an answer to a question. In this case, you should at least start to write something. If you have studied properly for the exam, you will definitely know something relevant. As Ralph Waldo Emerson said, "We are wiser than we know." Try to think of the general themes and major points you studied to see if they are somewhat germane to the question. As you start to write, you will find that information starts to return. Sometimes you will connect with a memory chain in which one thought reminds you of another thought, and so on, until you have a fairly decent answer to the question. One thing is certain: If you write nothing you will not get any credit. If you write *something* there is at least a chance to score some points, even if what you have written is fragmentary.

If the approaches I have suggested do not work and you hit an absolute impasse, do not spend too much time on the question. Allow some extra space in your exam booklet for the answer and move on to the next question. You can return to the troublesome question toward the end of the exam, after you have finished the more manageable questions. By this time, you may be more prepared to handle it, because your mind has had additional time to work on the problem on a subconscious level.

Another factor to recognize is that you are bound to make some mistakes on exams. Nobody is perfect. You may have started to answer the question in the wrong way. Or even if you started to answer it correctly, you may have gotten off the track. You have to be very cautious as you work to detect such problems. If you catch yourself committing such an error at an early point, you can always go back and correct it. According to John Maynard Keynes, the English economist, "There is no harm in being sometimes wrong—especially if one is promptly found out."

Perhaps the most disturbing thing to happen in an essay exam is to find you have run out of time. You may have been busy at work and lost track of time, when suddenly the teacher announces that all exam papers will be collected in five minutes! It is especially exasperating when you know the answers to the other questions, but it seems that you will never get a chance because you have not budgeted your time wisely. What should you do?

First of all, don't panic! The best approach is to supply an outline for the unanswered questions. List the major headings, subheadings, and supporting facts. Write a short note to your instructor explaining that you are supplying an outline because you have run out of time. You can often salvage most of the points in a question using this technique, because instructors realize that anyone can run out of time; they have probably done it many times themselves.

Objective Exams

Objective tests include true-false, multiple choice, fill in the blanks, and matching questions, or some combination of these forms. A test is called objective if the same standards and conditions apply to everyone taking the test and there is only one "right" answer to the question. Whereas essay exams require you to organize and present ideas in a logical fashion, objective tests primarily measure your ability to recall information. A well-designed objective exam can also test your ability to understand, analyze, interpret, and apply your knowledge, but it cannot test creativity.

Objective questions are frequently used in standardized examinations, but you will not encounter many in the college classroom. Some instructors would probably prefer to use objective exams because they are easy to grade and reduce the amount of their work. In spite of this, most instructors will not give an objective exam because such exams are felt to be superficial and mechanistic by both teachers and students alike. About the only place you will encounter them is in entry-level or very large classes where there is a heavy workload, and even there they are considered to be an embarrassment. Notwithstanding this, I will cover some of the basic principles of taking objective exams, should you encounter any.

The basic principles of taking an objective exam are different from those used in an essay exam. You should quickly look over the exam to see the number of questions and pages, but you should not try to read through all of the questions before marking your answers. The best approach is to answer the questions in the order they appear on the exam. Leave the more difficult questions blank, mark them with a question mark, and move on to the next question. You can return to these more difficult questions after you have finished the easier ones. They may be more manageable at a later point, since your mind has had additional time to consider them on a subconscious level. In addition, you might find information in other questions that will help you to answer the more difficult ones. Do not be superstitious about the pattern of responses. For example, don't be influenced by a pattern like T,F,T,F,T,F, ... , on a true-false test, or a,b,c,a,b,c, ... , on a multiple choice exam.

There are a few special principles to observe on multiple choice exams. These exams are sometimes challenging because there are often several choices that seem plausible, and it is difficult to choose the correct one. The best approach is to try to determine the answer before you look at the options. If you see the answer you guessed, you should still examine the other options to make sure that none seem "more correct" than your guess. If you do not know the answer, read each option very carefully and eliminate the options you know to be wrong. That way, you can arrive at the correct answer through a process of elimination.

There is a lot of folk wisdom about taking objective exams, based principally on the assumed naïveté of your instructor—which may not be the case! For example, some would advise you to avoid options which use words like *all, none, always, never, must, only,* and so on, because nothing in life is so exclusive. They advise you to choose options which use words that allow for some exception, such as *sometimes, frequently, rarely, often, usually, seldom, normally,* and so on. They also advise you to avoid the first and last option, because instructors feel more comfortable about putting the correct answer in the middle. Another recommendation offered is to select the option that is either shorter or longer than the rest, because it is more likely to be correct. Some would advise you to never change an answer, since your first intuition is usually correct.

Although there may be a grain of truth in this folk wisdom, it is basically superstition and you should avoid it! If you want some advice, listen to Benedict Spinoza, the great Dutch philosopher: "He who would distinguish the true from the false must have an adequate idea of what is true and false."

Here is some additional advice to follow. If you have gone all of the way through the exam and you still do not know the answer to a question, then guess. That's right, guess. At least you have a chance of being correct—a very good chance on a true-false test and a decent chance on a multiple-choice test. Even on exams where there is a penalty for being wrong, it still pays to guess if the penalty is small enough. As President Franklin D. Roosevelt once advised a group of students, "It is common sense to take a method and try it. If it fails, admit it frankly and try another. But above all, try something."

Problem Exams

Problem exams are used mainly in the quantitative disciplines, such as mathematics and the sciences, to test your ability to use logical reasoning to solve problems. Some people have a mental block against mathematics in any form, commonly known as "math anxiety." They "freeze-up" at the very thought of having to take a math test. The ability to do mathematics is tied to your ability to reason abstractly, which, to some degree, is innate. Some view mathematics as an art form. Listen to Bertrand Russell, a philosopher and mathematician: "Mathematics, rightly viewed, possesses not only truth, but supreme beauty—a beauty cold and austere, like that of sculpture." He was referring mainly to pure, abstract mathematics. Even if one is not by nature a mathematician, there are a few basic principles that will help you to score higher on problem tests.

As in essay tests, you should read through all of the problems before you start to answer any one. As you read each question, underline key words that tell you what to do and important data, such as given information, units of account, and so on. In the margin of your paper, jot down any thoughts that come to mind, such as specific formulae or possible approaches for solving the problem. Move quickly to the next problem and continue with the same procedure. After you have read all of the questions, you will have a good idea of the ones that will be relatively easy and those that could cause some difficulty. If you have a choice, select the problems that will give you the least trouble and figure out how much time you will have to work on each one. Work on the easiest problems first and return to the more difficult ones later, for the same reasons discussed in the previous section on essay exams.

As you go back to work each problem, make sure that you have an exact knowledge of what is being requested. List the unknowns so you will know what you are trying to solve. It may be helpful to organize the given data in a table or draw a picture or diagram that shows what you will need to do to solve the problem. If possible, try to predict a reasonable answer to the problem before starting to work, to provide a basis for comparison later on. Always show all of your work on problem exams, rather than trying to make complex computations in your head. If you make a stupid mistake and get an incorrect answer, the teacher can see where you went wrong and at least give you partial credit. Be very careful and deliberate about your calculations, as it is easy to make computational errors. Make sure that your answer meets all of the requirements of the problem. After you have finished your work, draw a box around your answer to make it easier to locate.

Unfortunately, things do not always—or, rather, usually do not—go so smoothly. You will encounter problems that are extremely difficult to solve. After all, isn't that what problem tests are all about—testing your wits? What should you do in such cases?

If a problem is very difficult to solve, you may have to approach it in a different manner. First, think about similar problems from class or homework and the methods that were used to solve them. Very often there will be a clever substitution or particular approach that will make the problem easier to solve. Remember that there is often more than one way to solve a problem and, also, several wrong ways. You may have to attack the problem from several different angles to obtain the correct answer. The main thing is to keep working on the problem because you know that a correct answer exists. If you are only able to solve part of the problem, write it down, at least you will get partial credit.

Open Book Exams

Some instructors prefer open-book examinations, in which the student is allowed to use supplementary materials such as notes, textbooks, charts, or "crib sheets." Some instructors place restrictions on the materials allowed for the exam, while others allow you to use anything you wish. The open-book exam measures the student's ability to organize and present ideas, as well as locate information necessary to answer the questions.

Why would an instructor want to give an open-book exam? Open-book exams are often used where there is an excessive amount of detailed material that would be unreasonable to expect the student to remember. They also are used in courses where charts or tables are needed to look up information to answer the questions, such as mathematics and science classes. Some instructors feel that you should be allowed to use supplementary materials in any exam, because you will have access to these materials when solving problems in the working world.

It should be clearly recognized that an open-book exam does not absolve you of the need to study or prepare for the exam. You can have access to all of the materials imaginable, but they will be of little value if you don't know how to use them. The situation is similar to what Voltaire, the French author, referred to as "the embarrassment of riches." You may have so many materials that you do not know what to do with them. That is why it is important to read your books and learn how to use the charts, tables, and formulae before the test. You should be very familiar with these materials if you have kept up with your assignments during the semester. You should study for an open-book exam using the same methods as for other in-class exams, as I will discuss in Part Three.

If your instructor allows you to use a "crib-sheet" during the exam, prepare a well-organized sheet that contains essential information. If you try to write down everything imaginable, your summary will be next to useless. Besides, it is probably physically impossible to summarize all of the material covered by a test on a single sheet of paper. You may find it helpful to use your "crib-sheet" as an index, to point to the relevant places in the text or lecture notes containing information on a particular topic.

You should make sure that you know exactly which materials may be used during the exam. It could be very disconcerting to come to class without a book needed for the test or, worse yet, to find out that you cannot use a book you had planned on using. If the teacher allows you to use these materials during the exam, don't be haughty and scorn them because you think you know it all. These materials are important tools that will help you to accomplish your task; and besides, why put yourself at a disadvantage compared to your classmates?

Take-Home Exams

The take-home exam is essentially an open-book exam, but with more time allowed for the student to complete the test in his own surroundings. Most instructors give you at least a week to work on the exam and allow you to use any materials you wish. Because of the extra time allowed, the instructor has to make the take-home exam more difficult than the in-class exam, or everyone would get an A. I always disliked take-home exams because of their length and complexity. I preferred in-class exams because I felt that my system of study gave me an edge over the other students, and they required less time and work to complete than take-home exams. Fortunately for the student, take-home exams have lost some of their popularity. Some professors also have realized that it takes them much longer to grade a take-home exam than an in-class exam.

Why would an instructor want to give a take-home exam? One reason is to aid certain kinds of students. Sophocles once remarked, "To him who is in fear everything rustles." There are some students who have a psychological barrier to taking exams in class, so they are never quite able to demonstrate what they know. These students become "rustled" at the very thought of taking exams in class under a fixed-time limit. The take-home exam gives the instructor another independent reading of the students' abilities. Take-home exams also are occasionally used if the subject material is very complex or extensive, and additional time and space are needed to test in-depth mastery.

A significant mistake often made by students is that they do not allow themselves enough time to complete take-home exams. They tend to procrastinate until the last few days before the exam, and then they panic. You should try to start working on your take-home exam at the earliest possible convenience. Divide the total amount of time to complete the exam by the number of questions, and allot yourself this much time to answer each of the questions. Do your best to stick to this schedule and avoid the temptation to procrastinate.

Because of the complexity of take-home exams, you will likely have to look beyond your lecture notes and textbooks to outside readings in order to answer some of the questions. This is another reason why you should start working on the exam as soon as possible. The sources listed on the reading list handed out by the instructor are a good place to start your research for answers to the questions on a take-home exam. Now that you know how to read a book effectively, you can scan these sources to find those containing material relevant to the questions. Don't forget that some of the answers may be located in your lecture notes.

In writing your answers to the questions on a take-home exam, you should use basically the same writing principles discussed in the chapter "How to Write A Term Paper." There is one key difference, however. In the take-home exam you should make your answers very concise and to the point, whereas term papers are supposed to reflect extensive research. Remember the principle of "Ockham's razor" when writing your answers. Put the answers in your own words rather than stitching together a series of quotations from the readings.

Finally, it is a good idea to type the answers to the questions if possible. Your instructor will appreciate the fact that you are making life a little easier, and may even reward you with a slightly higher grade.

Oral Exams

Oral exams are often given as a final test before awarding a degree, such as an undergraduate degree in an honors program or an advanced degree in a graduate program. They are like "rites of passage" at different stages of the college career. The custom dates back to Medieval times before the invention of the printing press, when exams had to be given orally. Despite the prevalence of printing today, the custom has survived largely because university adminstrations feel that true scholars should also possess oratorical skills. As Ben Jonson, a 17th-century English dramatist, once said, "Talking and eloquence are not the same; to speak, and to speak well, are two things. A fool may talk, but a wise man speaks."

The typical setting in an oral exam is for the student to answer questions about the subject matter or defend a piece of work before a committee of several professors. For example, I had to defend my Ph.D. dissertation before six professors and a dean as part of the requirement for my degree. Orals which test your ability in the subject matter are much more extensive, often requiring in-depth knowledge about an entire field or curriculum. Because of the importance of these exams for passing on to the next stage of your career, it is imperative that you be ready.

You should take several steps to get ready for your big oral exam. Rely heavily on your adviser to help you prepare for the exam. It is in your adviser's interest for you to succeed, to enhance his or her own reputation for successfully developing students. Talk to your adviser beforehand to obtain information on the scope of the exam, and what the experience will be like. Ask about the background and orientation of the other professors on the committee, and whether they have any pet theories or axes to grind that you should be knowledgeable about. Practice rehearsing answers to probable questions, either by yourself or with other students. If possible, go to the examination room beforehand and notice details about the room, such as where people will sit and the temperature—so you can wear comfortable clothing.

In other words, check out everything in advance so you will not be surprised when you arrive to take the exam.

Oral examinations measure your ability to analyze and integrate information and to respond quickly in an organized manner. There are several pointers that will help you to do this more effectively. Always listen very carefully to your examiner's questions so you will know what is being requested. If you do not fully understand the question then ask for a clarification. As the question is being asked, you should start to think about your answer, so you can respond promptly in an organized manner. Look directly into your examiner's eyes when giving your answer, speak in an affirmative tone, and be sure to use proper technical terms and pronunciation to demonstrate that you have mastered the material.

What do you do if the instructor asks a question that you are not knowledgeable about? If you do not immediately know the answer, it is better to say something rather than sit there with a blank stare on your face. As Francis Bacon once noted, "Silence is the virtue of fools." Talk about related information that you do know, and maybe you will hit on a memory chain that will lead you to the correct answer. If you think of an answer to a previous question that initially stumped you, then mention it at a convenient point.

The most important thing to realize is that orals are just another test in a slightly different form. The major difference between oral and written exams is that you are using your mouth rather than the pen in your hand to respond. No one is out to destroy you or prevent you from achieving your goal. There is nothing inherently more unnerving about an oral exam than any other type of exam. In fact, oral exams actually have some advantages over written exams. If you give an answer that is off the mark, you have an opportunity to modify and expand your response. In general, you will use essentially the same study methods to prepare for an oral exam as in any other exam, as decribed in Part Three. Just try to relax, keep a cool head, and look forward to a new experience.

Comprehensive Written Exams

The comprehensive exam is the written counterpart to the oral exam which covers your knowledge about an entire field or curriculum. Many departments require comprehensive examinations at the end of a program to ensure that the student has achieved a certain level of mastery of the subject. The practice is much more common among graduate programs than undergraduate programs. For example, I did not have any comprehensive exams as an undergraduate but I had to take four full-day comprehensive exams in economics as part of the requirement for my Ph.D. degree. Although, as Virgil said, "We are not all capable of everything," the comprehensive exam is the one situation where you are expected to know just about everything

Taking comprehensive exams can be very tricky. I took one in which I missed a number of questions and another in which I had correct answers to practically all of the questions. The second comprehensive was an extension of the material covered in the first comprehensive, indicating that I really had mastered the material presented in the first exam. It is difficult to predict in advance exactly what you will be up against when taking comprehensive exams.

Perhaps the most important aspect of the comprehensive exam is the person (or persons) making up the test. If the *only* person making up the test is the instructor you had for the course, then you are in very good shape. In this case, you can use the standard methods to prepare for the exam that I will discuss in Part Three. On the other hand, if several persons are making up the test, then you will need to do some extra work. Different instructors stress different content in the classroom, even on the same subject, and sometimes use different books and articles. In this case, your best bet is to talk to the other instructors to find out what they covered in class.

They may be willing to give you a reading list, their lecture notes, or other helpful materials.

In preparing for comprehensive exams, you should try to "look at the forest before inspecting the trees." Make an effort to identify the major themes running through the various courses. It is not necessary to go back and read extensively for details; this may even interfere with your ability to integrate information. After you have identified the major themes, then you can flesh them out with additional details. Develop a definite point of view and think about the questions that might be asked on these themes and how you would answer them.

It may be a good idea to review past comprehensive exams to obtain a feel for the nature and scope of the questions. Many departments keep copies of old exams in the library as reference materials. You should think about the way you would respond to these questions, but don't actually write your answers out since questions rarely appear on exams more than once.

The major consideration about comprehensive exams is that you will need to expend some extra effort to make sure there are no gaps in your knowledge. This is not a problem, in most cases, since you will normally have several months to prepare for your comprehensive exams. The familiar advice about avoiding procrastination still applies.

Well, that just about sums up the strategies for taking different kinds of exams.

There is one more topic in this chapter that needs to be covered. Just as there are basic principles to follow before taking tests, there are other basic principles to follow during tests. I am sure that you also have heard these at least a thousand times, but they are violated just as often. Read them carefully!

Basic Principles During the Test

Write clearly. You can increase the odds of doing well on an exam by writing your responses to the exam questions in a clear fashion. Go out of your way to write neatly and organize your responses as carefully as possible. Your instructor is more likely to understand your answer if you use good penmanship and practice the rules of good grammar, spelling, paragraph construction, and theme development. As George Orwell, the English author, once noted, "Good prose is like a window pane." This point is irrelevant if you are taking an objective exam, but most college exams tend to have essay questions. I find that I can write essays more neatly by using a pencil rather than a pen, because I can go back and erase parts if I change my mind—which invariably happens.

Put yourself in your instructor's place. There are probably many other things that you would rather do than grade a huge number of exams. In most cases, it is like watching several reruns of a below-average movie. Since grading exams is an inherently unpleasant task to the instructor, it is worth your extra effort to make your responses easy to read.

I can remember one instance where an instructor told me that he added five extra points to my exam score because my answers were written so neatly. Although few teachers would be willing to admit this openly, I think that the same phenomenon is operative with most instructors, and it may be on a subconscious level.

Remember, if you do a sloppy job on answering the exam questions, you will only give the impression that you do not know the complete answer to the question. Contrary to what some students think, teachers will not give them a break simply because their writing is illegible. The teacher is more likely to miss the gist of your answer if it is put down illegibly. Although it takes more effort and care to write neatly, it will pay handsome dividends. As Titus Maccius Plautus, the Roman dramatist, said, "Write it down in a good firm hand."

Review your answers. If you finish answering the questions on an exam ahead of time, go back and review your answers. It is very easy to make a careless mistake if you are writing rapidly. Even if you have tried to be careful, your essays may be filled with poor grammar, faulty spelling, faulty paragraph construction, illegible writing, and so on. In an objective test, you may have been guilty of clerical errors. In a problem test, you may have made a logical error or a computational mistake. You can catch many of these careless errors by using the remaining time to carefully review your answers. As the ancient Greek dramatist, Euripides, said, "In this world second thoughts, it seems, are best."

As you re-read your answer in an essay exam, ask yourself if you really have given a good answer to the question. Supplement your answer with other thoughts that come to mind during your review. You will find that you are often able to come up with additional information or new ideas if you have left your answer alone for a while. Make sure that you have used complete sentences and that your thoughts come across clearly. This will help to give your answer a more finished and polished look, and will increase your total point score.

In practically every examination I have ever taken, some students invariably finish ahead of time and turn their paper in before the final call. Either they knew too little and could not finish the exam, or they were very self-confident and thought they knew too much. Perhaps they were trying to impress the teacher or other students about how much they knew. Sometimes you can hear them cursing out in the hall or before the next class about the information they knew all the while but forgot to write on their exam paper!

It is stupid to use less than the total amount of time allotted for an exam. Any product can be made better with additional work and an exam is no exception. Don't turn in your exam paper until you are told to leave the classroom.

Never cheat. I shouldn't even have to mention this one, but I will because it is violated all of the time. Some students use "crib sheets" during a closed book exam and others attempt to read answers from their classmates' papers. Cheating is stupid because (a) you might get caught, and (b) you are implicitly assuming that someone else knows a better answer than you do. If you have been following my system, you probably know as much as anyone in the classroom, so trust yourself. If you're still not convinced, think of the consequences of being caught. In addition to being embarrassed, you might get an F in the test or the course, or be expelled if the school has a tough policy.

And finally, even if you succeeded in cheating, you would not have a feeling of accomplishment, because you did not earn your grade fairly.

Well, that concludes a rather lengthy chapter on "How to Take a Test." If you have understood everything I have presented you now have the knowledge to become a test-wise student—but more is required. In order to become a test-wise student you have to practice these principles. As Publilius Syrus, the Roman philosopher, said 2,000 years ago, "Practice is the best of all instructors."

PRINCIPLE 2
A test-wise student knows the methods for taking various types of exams and practices them continually.

3

HOW TO WRITE A TERM PAPER

Now that you know something about the art of reading and thinking, let's concentrate on the art of writing.

As a form of communication, writing is just as essential in our society as speaking. Our everyday activities involve writing of some kind, whether it is a letter written to a friend, a note written to a relative, a report written for a school assignment, or a memorandum prepared at work. Much of the communication in the business world is written rather than verbal, in order to provide a more permanent record of events.

Think about it for a minute. Can you remember just one day in your life when you did not write anything? Probably not.

Writing is the most important form of communication you will have with your instructors in college. It is the major means of communication not only in English composition or literature, but in all of your courses. Your grade in a course is determined largely by what you write on exams. In addition, many courses have other written assignments, such as essays, reports, themes, book reviews, and term papers. Next to reading, writing will demand more of your time as a student than any other activity.

Despite the importance of writing, it is a skill that is not well developed in the general population. Many adults in the working world lack the ability to write well, and this is one of the major obstacles preventing them from advancing further in an organization. Many college students have a negative attitude toward writing because it is difficult for them. For some, writing has always been a problem because they never learned the basic principles of composition in primary and secondary school. In fact some people have already given up, concluding that they just cannot write well.

Of the various written assignments in school, the term paper is one of the most important—and also one of the most troublesome—to students. A lengthy term paper can account for a third or more of your total grade. You probably have known many students, perhaps yourself included, who have avoided taking a course because a term paper was required. I have been guilty of this myself. Many students do not like term papers because they involve an extensive amount of work and time to complete—time that could be used to study material in other courses or prepare for exams. And even if the student spends the time and effort writing the paper, there is no guarantee that it will be successful. As Aldous Huxley , the English critic, remarked, "A bad book is as much of a labor to write as a good one; it comes as sincerely from the author's soul."

Why would instructors put students through all of the trouble to write a term paper? Is it intended as punishment? No, that's definitely the wrong attitude.

Your instructor knows that writing a term paper is a way for you to develop skills that will be needed later in life, regardless of the occupation you decide to enter. Writing a term paper requires you to examine a particular topic in detail. You have to demonstrate that you know how to use appropriate research methods to investigate the topic. You also will have to know how to use the various resources in the library to gather information related to the topic. Next, you have to organize and synthesize this information to address the topic.

Finally, you have to present your findings in a well-written and carefully documented paper. These are the basic steps that a scholar goes through to write a book or article, but they are also the steps that a researcher in any field must go through to examine a topic.

Another reason why some instructors assign term papers is to obtain another independent look at the students' abilities. Since some students perform poorly on exams with a fixed time limit, the term paper affords them an opportunity to demonstrate their capabilities under a different format.

Okay, you have just been given an assignment to write a term paper in one of your classes. How do you proceed?

Select a topic. The first task is to select a topic for your term paper. Since you will be spending a lot of time and effort conducting research for the paper, you should definitely choose a topic in which you are interested. Your selection may be a subject in which you have always been interested or it may be on something intriguing which was discussed during a lecture. If the instructor has assigned a topic, then you obviously do not have any choice; however, most instructors allow the student at least some leeway.

Try to limit your topic to something fairly specific, because it may become unmanageable to handle if it is too broad. Avoid very general, vague, or controversial topics that are impossible to deal with in the space and time available to write the paper. If you are having difficulty limiting your topic at the outset, which is not unusual, select a general topic but remember to narrow it as your research progresses.

Selecting a good topic is particularly important when writing a master's thesis or a doctoral dissertation in a graduate program. Considering the amount of work required, you should select a topic that you find extremely interesting and for which there is a possibility to make a significant contribution. You have to feel that the topic is important to make a contribution; if you don't have this feeling, then select another topic.

Develop relevant questions. George Moore, the English philosopher, once wrote, "It appears to me that . . . difficulties and disagreements . . . are mainly due to a very simple cause:

namely to attempt to answer questions, without first discovering precisely *what* question it is which you desire to answer."

You should attempt to develop specific questions, and identify relevant issues, that you want to address in your term paper. Write these down on a piece of paper. They may be very broad at this point, but they will at least provide a starting point for organizing thoughts as you conduct your research.

Conduct your research. Now that you know the relevant questions and issues, how do you go about conducting research?

Your instructor is a primary source of information for locating key reading materials to start you on your effort. Some of these sources will probably be listed in your course outline. If you need additional sources, ask your instructor to recommend other books and articles that are relevant to your topic. Each reading source will have references that will provide leads for additional reading materials.

You should also use the resources in the library to obtain additional reference materials. As you look through the card catalogue for books and articles that you already know about, you can locate other entries that seem relevant to your topic. A more efficient method for locating sources is to use a computerized bibliographic search system, if one is available at your library. Using a few key words, these systems can locate additional books and articles, not only in your library but in others as well. Many of these systems provide a useful printout containing a brief synopsis of the content, which will help you to determine if the source is relevant to your topic. In general, you should plan to use various resources in the library, including books, articles, encyclopedia, reference books, and the librarian, when necessary. As Samuel Johnson once noted, "A man will turn over half a library to make one book."

As you review these sources, use the methods discussed in the previous chapter on "How to Read a Book" to determine if the source is relevant to your topic. By scanning the table of contents, summaries, and headings, you should not have to take more than a few minutes to make a determination.

If a work is relevant to your topic, take very careful notes as you read. The objective is to record relevant information, not everything you read. As William James said, "The art of being wise is the art of knowing what to overlook." If you read something that you want to quote, then designate it with quotation marks, and check what you have written to make sure it is accurate. Some people take notes verbatim from books they are reading and put the thoughts into their own words later, while writing the paper. I prefer to translate the author's thoughts into my own words while taking notes, because the information is more meaningful to me that way. In addition, I avoid the task of translation later, when the thought is not as clear. Whether you are quoting or translating another person's thoughts, you will need to keep track of relevant information for references and citations. Make sure that you record relevant bibliographic information, such as the title of the book, name of the author, publishing house, where and when it was published, and the page number. It's time consuming and no fun to look up these details at a later time.

Everyone seems to have their own system for recording information during the research phase. Some individuals use elaborate index card systems, such as $3'' \times 5''$ cards for bibliographic information and larger cards for taking notes. Others, like myself, record information on plain notebook paper. It doesn't matter which system you use, as long as it makes you feel comfortable and you use it systematically. One recommendation is worth noting. Write only on one side of the page because it is easier to spread everything out to see what you have. It can become very messy and confusing when you have written on both sides.

It is very important to read extensively if you are going to come up with some new thoughts from a synthesis of the various sources. Good research is more than demonstrating that you have mastered what others have already shown; you should attempt to do something new.

Easier said than done, right? Yes, that's true, but you can at least create an environment which encourages creative thinking.

Creative thinking involves several stages. The first stage is to recognize the question as clearly as you can, which you have already done. The next stage is to accumulate as much knowledge as you can about the question; immerse yourself in it! This essentially is what you are doing when reading every resource you can find on the subject of your term paper. The next stage is to leave the problem alone and let it incubate in your subconscious mind. Your conscious mind is not considering the problem but your subconscious mind is busy at work, coming up with new approaches and solutions to the problem. Some day when you are least expecting it, an ingenious insight will "pop into your head"—the product of creative thinking. All you need to do now is to compare it against the question asked in the first stage to see if it is a good solution.

Be sure to record these little gems of wisdom in your notes, for they often disappear as rapidly as they arrived.

As you conduct your research, your original questions may have changed, or at least become more specific. That's entirely natural, because it was impossible to come up with specific questions before conducting your research. The next step is to impose some structure on this mountain of material you have collected.

Develop an outline. An outline will help you to order your thoughts and develop a foundation to write a good paper. As noted by Edmund Burke, an English statesman, "Good order is the foundation of all good things."

As you conducted your research, you undoubtedly noticed that the information is grouped in some logical fashion. The grouping may have been in chronological order, geographical order, numerical order, in order of importance, or in order of complexity. You can see these groupings more clearly if they are organized in an outline.

All of us have learned how to construct an outline from our early years of schooling. The title of your paper will appear as the title of your outline. Major topics are designated by Roman numerals and subtopics are designated by capital letters, indented under the major topics. Further divisions of subtopics are possible, by using Arabic numerals, small letters, and so on, all with the appropriate level of indentation. When organized in this fashion, the outline serves as a blueprint to guide the structure and pattern of your thoughts. The outline helps you to clearly see the arrangement of the material, to check the balance between major and minor topics, to check for repetition and contradiction, and to facilitate the development and expression of new ideas.

After you have developed an outline, which sometimes takes time, index all of the notes from your readings to specific parts of the outline. In other words, write the number or letter of the corresponding topic from the outline on the appropriate pages containing your notes. This develops a link to tie all of the information together. You are now ready to:

Write your first draft. How does one start writing? Here is some advice from Samuel Eliot Morison, the American historian: "A few hints as to literary craftsmanship may be useful to budding historians. First and foremost, *get writing!*"

That's right. Sit down at your desk or typewriter, get out your outline and notes, take out some blank paper, and start writing.

The beginning, or introduction, is important because it is where you will state your central theme and attempt to encourage your reader to continue reading. You should avoid lengthy introductions because, if you have succeeded, your reader will be anxious to get into the work.

Just because the introduction is short does not mean that it will be easy. As Blaise Pascal, the French philosopher, said, "The last thing one knows in constructing a work is what to put first." It is very difficult to get something down on paper at the start to meet all of the requirements of a good introduction. Some writers would encourage you to write the introduction last, after you already know how the paper has turned out. However, I would encourage you to get something down on paper at the outset, even if you have to trash it several times. This will at least give you additional time to work on different approaches.

To write the middle, or the body, of your paper, all you have to do is to merge your notes into the outline. The major topics in the outline become the major chapters or headings in the paper. The subtopics in the outline become minor headings within the chapters or major headings. The notes from your readings flesh out the body of the paper under each of these headings. Make sure that your major and minor headings stand out and display the proper hierarchical order.

This is not the place to review the fundamentals of good writing—that's why you take courses in English composition in high school and college. However, a few major points are in order. As you write your paper, remember the fundamentals of good paragraph construction. The first or second sentence, known as the topic sentence, states the major idea in the paragraph. Additional sentences illustrate or support that point through the use of facts, examples, statistics, and so on. Your reader will be looking for some concrete evidence to support your statement. Your paragraphs should be presented in a logical fashion to develop your theme. Remember to include transitions between the paragraphs so the presentation flows smoothly. In addition, vary the length of paragraphs, and sentences within paragraphs, so your writing will not be monotonous.

I refer you to your textbooks in English I for additional details on the fundamentals of good writing.

Finally, the ending of your paper will contain a conclusion that summarizes your major findings. It should refer back to the introduction and address any important questions raised there. The conclusion should cast the findings in a broader light in terms of their implications and the need and direction for further research. It will contain the final thought that you will leave with the reader.

Try to write the first draft of your paper as close to the final product as possible, to reduce the amount of future revision. Observe the proper mechanics of writing in the construction of paragraphs and sentences and the spelling of words. Make citations at the appropriate places. You may find that writing at a fairly rapid rate will produce a smoother, more evenly flowing version that will be closer to a final product. If, in the process of writing, you find a better way to express your thoughts, modify your outline as necessary.

After you finish your first draft, let it sit for a while. This lapse usually helps you to come up with new ideas or approaches to strengthen your presentation. You are now ready to—

Write your final version. What? Write another version? And you thought you were finished! Even though your first version may have looked very good initially, you will undoubtedly see many flaws after a careful inspection at a later date. Even accomplished writers occasionally find it difficult to write polished prose. Dale Carnegie, author of one of the most popular books ever written, used to say, "It was easier to make a million dollars than to put a phrase into the English language." And Mr. Carnegie ought to know, because his book, *How to Win Friends & Influence People*, sold millions of copies and made millions of dollars—in addition to adding a phrase to the language.

Although many writers dislike the task of rewriting, this phase can make the difference between a rough work and a polished work. It is similar to the process an artist goes through in painting a picture. The artist applies a first coat of paint which lays out the basic forms, such as mountains and rivers in a landscape scene. Although we can recognize these shapes at this stage, we know that the painting is far from finished. The second coat of paint starts to fill in the details, and the process is subsequently repeated until the painting embodies the effect desired by the artist.

As with the painting, you may have to rewrite your paper several times until you are satisfied with the result. During this process, you will be pruning unnecessary text, sharpening the language, improving the flow of ideas, and refining the introduction and conclusion, among other things. If you approach this phase seriously, your eraser will be almost as active as your pencil. If necessary, you should be willing to rewrite large sections of text to achieve the desired effect. That's right, tear up your old version and write a new one if necessary. Why do we go to such effort? Samuel Johnson gave a good reason more than 200 years ago, "What is written without effort is in general read without pleasure."

Follow the basic style conventions. Even if you have written a brilliant analysis, your paper will be less effective if you do not adhere to the basic style conventions. Type your manuscript on one side of standard-size (8-½" by 11") white paper, and maintain adequate space on all four sides of the page for margins. Use the appropriate conventions for making citations and references, and follow these conventions consistently throughout the entire paper. Your college bookstore should have a number of style manuals which describe these conventions. One that is highly regarded is, Kate L. Turabian, *Student's Guide for Writing College Papers*, listed in my references.

Some instructors have their own conventions for term papers. If this is the case with your instructor, make sure that you follow these conventions. If you are told to put footnotes at the bottom of each page instead of at the back of the paper, then do it. If the teacher prefers a given format for making references, then observe it. These are small concessions on your part, and may have a significant effect on your grade.

Start your paper early. By this time, it should be very clear that you will need to start working on your paper as soon as possible in order to finish all of the steps I have outlined. There are no hard and fast rules about the amount of time that should be devoted to each of the steps. As a rough rule of thumb, I suggest that you spend about one-half of your time selecting a topic, developing relevant questions, and conducting research on the various sources. Use the second half of your time developing an outline, writing your first version, and rewriting a final version. If you don't start working on the first step shortly after the paper is assigned, then there will be less time available to complete the other steps. You will need all of the time you can get if you are to think creatively, come up with new ideas, and rewrite your paper in a polished form.

Students have a terrible tendency to procrastinate on term papers. I know, because I was one of the worst offenders. Many do all of their work at the end of the semester when they are supposed to be studying for exams. They become cramped for time, and, consequently, view the whole experience as a necessary evil.

I have known many students who had to take an incomplete in their course because they were unable to finish their term paper before the end of the semester. The task does not become any easier or more pleasant later on.

Don't fall into this trap. And don't say that you have "writer's block." If you sit down at your desk and start writing, then you will at least get something down on paper. As Samuel Johnson once remarked, "A man may write at any time, if he will set himself doggedly to it."

If you start writing your term paper early enough, you will find the experience to be quite enjoyable. It is very exhilarating to increase your knowledge about a subject, develop some new thoughts that extend knowledge, and express them in your own words. Listen to the advice of H. L. Mencken, the great American journalist, on the pleasures of writing: "To the man with an ear for verbal delicacies—the man who searches painfully for the perfect word, and puts the way of saying a thing above the thing said—there is in writing the constant joy of sudden discovery, of happy accident."

Remember—although it takes a large amount of time to write an excellent paper, it is a good investment that will benefit you later on. As Ralph Waldo Emerson observed, "What is excellent is permanent."

PRINCIPLE 3
To write a good term paper, select a topic, develop relevant questions, conduct research, develop an outline, then write and rewrite as necessary. Start early!

SUMMARY

PART TWO
LEARNING THE BASIC SKILLS

PRINCIPLE 1

An active reader previews a book before reading it, and continually asks the questions that lead to a full understanding of the author's message.

PRINCIPLE 2

A test-wise student knows the methods for taking various types of exams and practices them continually.

PRINCIPLE 3

To write a good term paper, select a topic, develop relevant questions, conduct research, develop an outline, then write and rewrite as necessary. Start early!

A System For Getting Straight A's

OVERVIEW OF THE SYSTEM

Education has been emphasized since at least the time of the ancient Greeks, and there are any number of study guides available, so how is it that I have been able to come up with a new system of study? Inventions are not always the discovery of something new, but often are a recombination of things that are old. As Samuel Johnson said, "New things are made familiar, and familiar things are made new." You will undoubtedly recognize many of the ten steps in my system as good study tips that you have heard before. The unique aspect is the way they are combined into an integrated system to show you exactly what to do to become a straight-A student.

Marcus Aurelius once said, "Look to the essence of a thing, whether it be a point of doctrine, of practice, or of interpretation." Well, the essence of my system is very simple: *Instructors test students only on material covered explicitly in classroom lectures or discussion.* I have found this principle invariably to be true, regardless of the instructor or discipline. It is almost like a code of ethics with instructors. They feel that it is unfair to question students on material that has not been presented in a classroom setting. Although some other study guides seem to recognize this basic principle, they fail to exploit it in any systematic way.

Why would instructors subscribe to this principle? Think about it for a minute. All teachers want to put their own personal imprint upon you. They believe, as Henry Adams said, that "A teacher affects eternity; he can never tell where his influence stops."

Your professor has spent a good part of his or her lifetime studying the concepts and principles of a particular discipline. Years of study and research have been spent in working and re-working these concepts and principles into a form that— in your instructor's mind—captures the essence of the subject. Instructors bring the full range and depth of their knowledge into the classroom lecture. They use the lecture to describe the techniques and approaches that they have found most useful for understanding a subject. The content of the lecture reflects not just one way of understanding the subject, but what your instructor feels is the best way. After studying a subject for so long, he does feel there is a best way! If you understand everything presented in the lecture, then your instructor will be impressed that you have mastered in one semester what it took him or her a lifetime to accumulate. That will get you an A every time!

Some readers are probably thinking at this moment that my basic premise is flawed, since they would argue that they have been tested on material not covered in class. Although this could have happened, it is an extremely rare event; teachers who plan to test students on material not explicitly covered in class will usually give an advance notice of their intentions. The more likely occurrence is that the material was presented or discussed in the classroom, but the student failed to hear or grasp it. Scientific studies have shown that human beings are not very good listeners. We retain only a small fraction of the material presented to us.

I can remember on occasion thinking that the instructor was testing material covered outside the classroom. But upon re-examination of my notes or discussion with other class members, I discovered that, indeed, the material had been presented in class.

If you accept my premise, then I can show you a simple integrated system that will enable you to digest and master almost all of the material presented in class. As you have probably been able to tell, since you are now an active reader, my system covers everything from selecting a course to making an A in that course. I have used this system on different subjects, undergraduate as well as graduate courses, and classes with limited and extensive reading lists. I can assure you that it works! I will lay out my system in ten easy-to-follow steps, so it will be easy for you to remember or to refer to later for a refresher.

1

PLAN A COURSE OF STUDY

In one of his works, W.S. Gilbert, the English poet, wrote,

> *When I went to the bar as a very young man,*
> *(Said I to myself—said I),*
> *I'll work on a new and original plan,*
> *(Said I to myself—said I).*

When you enter college, you should work on a "new and original plan" for your course of study.

The first thing you should try to do upon entering college is to decide on your major field of study. Some people seem to know the field they want to major in from a very early age. Others, like myself, know the general area they want to study, but are initially undecided on a particular field. Many people change their major several times during their college career. This can be costly beyond some point because different fields have different requirements, and you may find yourself in college for an extended period.

If you are undecided on a field of study, then I have some

tips that should be helpful. The most important factor is to select a field that will enable you to enter an occupation you find desirable. In my opinion, the most desirable jobs are those that are enjoyable to do and also pay well. Salary is the common denominator that we can all agree on, but what we enjoy is a variable that differs from individual to individual. As noted by Lucretius, the Roman philosopher, "What is food to one, is to others bitter poison." You should start thinking about the line of work you would like to pursue after graduation, because you will need to take the proper coursework to gain entry to that field.

If you were fortunate enough to find a summer job as a student, then you at least have some idea of what is entailed in working. Unfortunately, most of the available summer jobs are low-paying, not very interesting, and not reflective of professional-level work. You might find it more enlightening to talk to someone who has just entered the workforce or older friends who are in certain lines of work. Even if you do not have personal or vicarious experience about the working world, there are other ways to obtain information.

A number of Government publications contain information about different occupations. The U.S. Bureau of the Census produces several reports showing the earnings levels and personal characteristics of workers employed in various different occupations. The U.S. Bureau of Labor Statistics publishes reports showing projections of the labor force and the expected number of workers who will be employed in different occupations. These reports should be available in your college library. This is very important information for planning a career. It does not make good sense to train for an occupation that will not have many openings, or in which there are so many workers that wages will be bid downward.

The counseling center at your university is a good place to obtain information on the characteristics of different jobs and job availabilities. Many firms looking for entry-level workers work closely with counseling centers. Some firms offer on-the-job training programs in which the student can obtain experience and earn money at the same time. Some of these arrangements offer excellent opportunities and I encourage you to look into them.

If you cannot decide on a specific field for a major, then at least make an effort to decide on a general area of study. In some curricula, you have a lot of flexibility in the first two years. You will be fulfilling certain general requirements that will count towards a degree in any number of fields. You can make your decision on a major later without losing your investment in specific coursework.

When you first enter college, you should make a realistic assessment of your capabilities and limitations as a student. Be very candid with yourself about the fields that have given you difficulty in the past and about weaknesses in basic skills.

If you feel that you are not up to par on basic skills—such as reading, comprehension, and writing—then you may want to take a special course in a reading and study skills laboratory (if you are fortunate enough to have one at your university). Many of these laboratories have teaching machines which give you practice at reading faster and test your comprehension through a series of questions and answers on what you have read. They also have programmed texts designed to broaden your vocabulary, increase your comprehension, and improve your study skills. It is silly not to take advantage of these services, even if you are an above-average student.

Once you have decided on a field of study, normally you are assigned to an adviser in the department who will help you to develop a schedule of courses. Most college programs require a certain number of courses in a wide variety of fields, such as English, social studies, mathematics, sciences, and so forth. These course requirements and electives normally are taken during the first two years of study, to allow sufficient time for you to concentrate on your major field of study in the last two years.

In deciding on your electives, I strongly encourage you to take additional courses in writing. In addition to the basic required composition courses, most English departments offer courses in expository and creative writing. As I noted earlier, most people are lacking in the basic writing skills. John Sheffield, Duke of Buckingham, once said, "Learn to write well, or not to write at all." Now, that's a little extreme and, besides, you really do not have a choice. But one thing is certain: Good writing ability will help you express yourself on essay examinations in all of your courses and will help you well beyond your college career.

In planning your schedule of classes it is important to take courses in the proper sequence. Many of the higher-level courses require a knowledge of material presented in lower-level courses. It is similar to building a house—you need a proper foundation before you can erect the walls. Courses listed in your college catalogue should show prerequisites for taking the course. However, this may indicate a bare minimum of preparation rather than what is desirable. It is often a good idea to ask your adviser, instructors, or other students about the proper level of preparation for courses. If you try to take courses out of sequence, you are only making the situation unnecessarily difficult for yourself.

If you are weak or lack confidence in a particular subject matter, it may be a good idea to start with a very low-level course rather than an advanced course. This applies to students who have not taken courses in a subject for several years, and especially to adults returning to college after many years. Even if you did very well in algebra a couple of decades ago, this does not necessarily mean that you are ready to jump right into a calculus course. By taking lower-level courses first you will establish a good foundation and the higher-level courses will be easier to handle when you eventually take them.

If you enroll in a class that is very difficult, don't be stubborn and try to tough it out if the material really is over your head. Show a little humility and find the course appropriate to your present level of knowledge. As Confucius once said, "When you know a thing, to hold that you know it; and when you do not know a thing, to allow that you do not know it—this is knowledge."

You need to be especially cautious when choosing elective courses. You may have an interest in taking some obscure upper-level course in literature or philosophy, but first make sure that you are adequately prepared to handle the material. If you are not prepared, you may find yourself at a serious disadvantage when competing on examinations with other students who have literature or philosophy majors. It would be wise to take some lower-level courses for background before taking the upper-level course. If your school offers pass-fail options for electives, then you can be venturesome without endangering your grade-point average.

I advise you to avoid televised classes if possible. Televised classes were very popular when I was an undergraduate because it was a way to compensate for the shortage of instructors. They are still popular in some large universities, particularly in first- and second-year classes. Some educators prefer televised courses because an expert or pre-eminent lecturer can be made available to all students. Furthermore, there is the assurance that all students are exposed to the core of information regarded as fundamental for mastering a subject. On the other hand, I find that I am more easily distracted in televised classes, particularly when other students are talking. The whole experience seems very impersonal to me. More importantly, what are you going to do if you have a question that needs to be answered to understand the material?

Once you have planned a course of study, try to stick with it so you can advance toward your degree. You should recognize, however, that many students change their majors and their plans as they progress through college. If you decide that you are in the wrong field, then I encourage you to make a change. If you do not like a particular field of study, then it is unlikely that you would enjoy a career in that field. It does not make any sense to continue training in a field that will only bring you a lifetime of unhappiness. Too many people have already made that mistake.

Most of my remarks in this section apply to undergraduate programs, but some of my remarks apply to graduate studies as well. It would not be wise to take an advanced graduate seminar before taking the basic foundation courses, even if you are intensely interested in the subject. Knowledge about the proper sequence of courses is usually more pervasive in a graduate program and advisers tend to work more closely with students.

The most salient aspect of graduate-level study is that it requires a higher level of commitment than undergraduate study. The course material is considerably more difficult and the reading assignments are much more specialized and extensive. In addition, you can expect a higher level of competition for grades because your fellow students are usually among the brighter persons who have graduated from college. In summary, you will be required to do a lot of hard work, and only those with a keen interest in the subject should be enrolled in a graduate program.

PRINCIPLE 1
Plan a course of study.

2
CHOOSE YOUR INSTRUCTOR

It is very important to choose your instructor before you register for a class, regardless of the subject you are studying.

The quality of instructors varies considerably, as does any good or service purchased in the marketplace. Do not assume that all instructors are good, or even competent, merely because they are highly educated. Instructors vary in the extent of their knowledge, in their natural intelligence level and, most importantly, in their ability to express themselves. George Bernard Shaw recognized the importance of differences between people when he said, "There are only two qualities in the world: efficiency and inefficiency; and only two sorts of people: the efficient and the inefficient." Although this statement is a little extreme, I think you have the idea.

Some students automatically select instructors who are the so-called "big names"—persons who are very well known in their field. However, some college instructors have built their reputation on the basis of their research accomplishments, and view teaching as a necessary evil. In the "publish or perish" world of today's universities, some instructors spend most of

108

their time working in laboratories or poring over journals so they can write papers to keep their jobs, get promotions, and impress their peers. As a result, they put very little effort into the preparation of their lectures and expect you to do all the work instead. A good instructor will put much more effort into the preparation of his or her lecture than what you will have to exert to get an A in the course.

What are the qualities that you should look for in an instructor? You should look for a dedicated instructor who covers a large volume of substantive material, is fair-minded, and is a good communicator. Stay away from instructors who are difficult merely because they are poor communicators. By the same token, do not assume that the best teacher is the easiest teacher. Even though you might be able to get a good grade without doing much work, what are you going to do when you encounter a more difficult teacher in the next course in the sequence? Your best bet is to select a person who is an excellent instructor as well as an accomplished researcher.

Jacques Delille, the French author, said, "Fate chooses our relatives, we choose our friends." You should choose your teacher as you would choose a friend, because your teacher is your companion in learning.

Most college instructors are in their profession because they love to teach. Considering their high level of educational attainment, they could probably find a much better-paying job in the outside world. But they remain in the teaching world because they enjoy the intellectual challenge and the opportunity to impart knowledge to students. Although the instructor's job may appear quite easy, since only a few hours of teaching are required each week, this does not reflect the extraordinary amount of work expended preparing lectures and conducting research. Many instructors work long hours and make signfiicant sacrifices to help students master the subject. It should be clear from their actions that teachers are a friend rather than a foe in the learning process, since they have your interest at heart.

Now that you know what to look for in a teacher, how do you go about finding the right person? The other instructors and students know who the good instructors are; all you have to do is to figure out a way to extract the information from them. If you have an outgoing personality, you can make friends with other students and teachers who can tell you about the qualities of various professors. They can provide valuable "inside information" on the best professors and courses to take.

The most difficult time to obtain this knowledge is when you first enroll in college. You know few, if any, of the students and teachers. In this case, you may have to rely on student newsletters, which occasionally publish the results of student polls on the quality of teachers. You can certainly learn something from the successes and failures of others. You should be somewhat wary of information in a newsletter, however, because it may reflect the superficial views of students who give low marks to good teachers who are difficult and high marks to poor teachers who are easy or humorous. Ask other students to provide specific details on why they think an instructor is good or bad, so you can judge their rationale. Listen to the advice of others, but make the final decision yourself, based on your best judgment.

I have found the best source of information on instructors to be other instructors. In other words, I prefer "experts" over "one who has had experience." Instructors are better able to judge other instructors than students because they know the discipline. It is not always so easy to get the information from them, however, because they do not want to be undiplomatic by saying something negative about a colleague. Instructors are more likely to identify the good teachers than the poor ones.

If you are considering a specific instructor, it is probably a good idea to talk to this person before you register for the class. This will enable you to get to know him or her as a person and to find out some specific details about the class. Some instructors will make their course outline and reading assignments available, so you can find out more about the content of the course. You can find out if the instructor assigns homework or requires papers, which books are used in the course, how many examinations are given, and any number of other useful details. If you have time, you may even want to sit in on a trial lecture to get a feel for the teacher's abilities and the content of the course. If you do this background work, you will gain knowledge of what the instructor has to offer.

Remember, picking the right instructor is important! You would not open the yellow pages to find the name of a doctor to perform a serious operation on your body. You would not close your eyes when you purchase clothes from a department store. Do not close your eyes and rely on pot luck when you register for a course either.

The author Henry James once wrote, "Life being all inclusion and confusion, and art being all discrimination and selection, the latter, in search of the hard latent *value* with which it alone is concerned, sniffs round the mass as instinctively and unerringly as a dog suspicious of some buried bone."

Like the dog suspicious of some buried bone, sniff round the mass and follow--

---

PRINCIPLE 2
Choose your instructor.

3
NEVER MISS A CLASS

Never miss a lecture—never! The importance of this principle should be obvious, given that test questions will come only from the lecture. Your instructor uses the lecture to present the material that he or she thinks is important for understanding the course. As noted earlier, instructors bring the full range of their knowledge into the classroom and use the lecture to explain the concepts in a form understandable to students. Contrary to the expectation of many students, instructors are not trying to trap or trick them. Instructors are more concerned about what students know than what they do not know. If you can demonstrate mastery over everything presented in class, then you have done enough to get an A in the course.

You are running a risk when you miss a class, because the exam may include questions on material covered while you were absent. Most of the exams I took in college had three or four essay questions. If you missed one essay question, you made a B at best, and more likely a C. Don't be foolish and take a chance. As Louis Pasteur said, "In the fields of observation, chance favors only the mind that is prepared." What applied to scientific observation applies to test-taking as well. Don't take chances!

When I say never miss a class, that includes not missing even part of a class. Always make an effort to get to class on time and do not get up and leave early, or you will miss part of the lecture. If you are unlucky, the material you miss may show up later as a question on an exam. Instructors often use the first five minutes of class to make important announcements, and they often use the last five minutes to summarize what was covered in the lecture or make an assignment for future classes. And by all means, do not start packing up your belongings five minutes before the class is over so you can make a mad rush for the door when the bell rings.

Always maintain good manners in the classroom, because your behavior will influence the teacher's impression of you as a student. Arrive in class on time, be sincere, diligent, and anxious to learn during class, and depart on time in an orderly manner. As King Louis XVIII of France declared, "Punctuality is the politeness of kings." Although it may not seem fair, the impression you create may have an influence on the grade you receive, particularly if your grades are on the borderline.

A common mistake made by many students is to assume that they can miss a class and cover themselves by going over the reading assignment more closely. This can be a fatal assumption, because many instructors do not exclusively use the reading material to construct their lecture notes. Throughout my entire college career, I can't remember even one instructor whose lecture was based exclusively on material from the textbook. Many instructors have told me that their lecture notes are based on material they studied as a student, updated, of course, for significant developments in the field. Instructors may update their lecture notes based on a more recent textbook assigned for a course, but they are unlikely to completely rewrite their notes based on the new book. Therefore, the safest bet is to attend every class so you will have an exact knowledge of the material presented. Don't make assumptions about what teachers will or will not do.

Even if instructors based their lectures entirely on the readings, you would miss something significant by not attending class. Classroom lectures change you in some fundamental way. Your instructor introduces you to new ideas. You may leave the classroom with a different view of the world than when you entered. Learning continues outside the classroom and at times when you are not studying. Your mind will probably be reviewing and synthesizing this new material at various times during the day, even when you are involved in everyday activities. This learning experience may take place while you are getting dressed, eating, walking to class, or in any number of other situations. You may find yourself silently reciting new facts or working over new problems that your instructor discussed in class. If you do not attend class, then there is no opportunity for this kind of learning to take place. The ancient Greek philosopher, Heraclitus, said, "You can't step twice into the same river." Like the passing river, missed classes are forever gone, lost and lamented.

The worst possible time to miss a class is towards the end of the semester. Ironically, many students miss class during this period because their schedules are very tight and they are trying to get ready for finals. Some instructors use the last few lectures to review and outline the entire course, or to mention what will be important for the final exam. Some even go so far as to tell you questions that will be on the final, or at least the possible range of questions. Other instructors use the last lecture as a general question-and-answer period, and it is not uncommon for some of these questions to show up on the final. If you miss the last few lectures, you will be at a significant disadvantage in competing against your classmates on the final.

If you absolutely cannot attend a class, which to me means that you are on your deathbed, then ask the instructor or one of the better students in the class to lend you their notes. It is preferable if you can get the instructor's notes, but some are not willing to go this far to accommodate you. Rewrite the borrowed notes in your notebook. If you do not fully understand everything the instructor or student has written, ask for a clarification of the material. This should help you to keep up in the short run, but it is no way to operate in the long run.

Edmund Burke, the British statesman, said, "Example is the school of mankind, and they will learn at no other." Well, here is an example that you can use as a goal. During my entire graduate curriculum, I never missed or was late for one class. There were plenty of times when I had an excuse for missing class, but I resisted the temptation. I can remember going to class with the flu and a 104° fever. You might feel that this is total fanaticism, but I was concerned that the teacher might discuss material that would later be presented on a test. You will be surprised at what you can do, it you feel that you have to do it.

PRINCIPLE 3
Never miss a class.

4
ALWAYS SIT IN THE FRONT ROW

Emily Dickinson, the American poet, once wrote,

> *But, looking back—the First so seems*
> *To Comprehend the Whole—*
> *The Others look a needless Show—*
> *So I write—Poets—All—*

You are much more likely to "comprehend the whole" of your professor's lecture when you are sitting in the front row. You will absorb more of the material when in the front row because you will be oblivious to everything else going on in the classroom. All you will be able to see is the teacher and the blackboard, and you will absorb the nuance of every word and thought.

When you sit in the front row, the instructor knows that you are there to learn. The instructor is more likely to recognize you and learn your name, and think of you as a person rather than a name or a number on a sheet of paper. Classes in some universities have become so large and impersonal that the in-

116

structor never gets a chance to meet many of the students. It is very easy to feel, as Sophocles described the tragic character Oedipus, like a "stranger in a strange country."

Many people prefer to sit in the middle or back of the classroom because they feel vulnerable in the front row. They know that they will have less privacy in the front row, and the teacher will be more likely to call on them for a question. You have to be very attentive and sharp to sit in the front row, and that is precisely why you should sit there. You will get much more out of your lectures if you are awake and alive rather than in a daydream.

When you sit in the middle or back of the class, you are often distracted by the presence of other people—distracted by their movements, discussion, or mannerisms. If you sit further back in the lecture hall, you will find yourself daydreaming or unable to sit still. And as the philosopher Blaise Pascal once said, "I have discovered that all human evil comes from this, man's being unable to sit still in a room." That may be slightly overstated, but one thing is certain. When you sit near the back of the class it is often difficult to hear the instructor clearly, and the message often gets garbled. These distractions only create noise that will keep you from absorbing 100 percent of the material.

Do you know what they say about students in the average college class? They say that 10 percent are there because they really want to learn, another 10 percent don't have the slightest interest in what's going on, and the remaining 80 percent are engaged in sexual fantasies. You will find it much more difficult to have sexual fantasies in the front row, because there is nothing to see but the blackboard, and you have to be ready for the next question.

Some anonymous person once said, "Time flies when you are having fun." The phrase is most often used disparagingly to describe how slowly time seems to pass when you are being tortured. But the statement is true. I can remember going into a lecture and being so absorbed that when the lecture was over, I felt as it I had just walked into the classroom. I was so engrossed in what was going on that I completely lost track of time. I was not "spaced out"—but just "wired in" to everything the teacher was saying. When you start to feel this way, the whole learning experience becomes more enjoyable.

You have probably heard that humans typically use only a small fraction of their mental capacity. We can utilize much more of it by concentrating deeply, but we must be in an environment that is conducive to this type of activity. A passage in the Book of Job in the Bible inquires, "But where shall wisdom be found? and where is the place of understanding?" The place of understanding in the college classroom is in the front row, because that is where you will find the environment that helps to maximize your comprehension and retention of the material.

Now I know that with a class of 30 students or more, not everyone can sit in the front row. My experience, however, is that very few people want to sit in the front row, so it should be quite easy to find an available seat. Don't despair if the front row is completely filled by the time you get to class. In instances like this, your best bet is to sit as close to the front row as you can, in the second or third row if possible. Do the best you can with the circumstances at hand and avoid thinking or worrying about it. Make an effort to get to class earlier next time.

If you want to "comprehend the whole" of what your professor has to say, follow—

PRINCIPLE 4
Always sit in the front row.

5
COMPLETE YOUR ASSIGNMENT BEFORE GOING TO CLASS

If you are to be prepared for your next class, you will need to complete your homework assignment before attending it.

Homework assignments typically fall into two categories: written assignments and reading assignments. Written assignments provide your instructor with immediate information about how much work you have done and how well you have understood it. Although reading assignments do not provide immediate feedback to your instructor, they are just as important for understanding the subject. Reading assignments will determine how much you understand from the lecture and, ultimately, how well you will do in the course.

Your first task is to find out what is expected of you in the way of homework assignments. Most instructors will hand out a course outline which is a blueprint on how to learn. The outline will tell you what will be covered in the course over the duration of the semester, and what will be expected of you—and when it will be expected. In fact, the better-organized instructors often hand out an outline listing the reading and written homework assignments for each lecture. If your instructor has not provided an outline or reading schedule, you should try to make up one for yourself. You can easily ask your instructor at the end of a lecture about the material that you should read for the next lecture, or future lectures.

Most course outlines will also list the titles of the books and articles that you are expected to read during the semester. I strongly encourage you to purchase all of the textbooks required or recommended for a course. Your instructor has selected a particular textbook because he or she feels that it has an advantage over other books either in content or method of presentation. In all likelihood, it will be a useful introduction to the subject and complement the material presented by your instructor during lectures. After completing the course, you should retain your textbooks for future reference. Of the various books on a subject, the book that you used for the course is probably the one you are most comfortable with and knowledgeable about.

I have some additional advice about textbooks. It is not enough to buy them, you have to read them. As Mark Twain once said, "The man who does not read good books has no advantage over the man who can't read them."

When should you read your assignment? As you can tell by the title of this chapter, you should read your assignment before the next class. If you obtain nothing else from this chapter but that one thought, then the chapter will have been a success.

Completing the reading assignment before class will familiarize you with the material and make it easier to comprehend and retain when the instructor presents it in class. By scheduling your reading in this manner, you will find that your class lectures are more interesting and exciting, and that you are better able to organize and digest the material presented in class. You will be a more active listener during the lecture because you already know something about the subject.

Do you remember the saying by Euripides, the ancient Greek dramatist, that, "In this world second thoughts, it seems, are best"? Well, it is so much easier for the mind to process material the second time around, because it has already resolved many of the problems and questions initially encountered.

If you have not resolved these problems from your first reading of the material, then the classroom is an excellent place to raise your questions. You can bring up these questions before, during, or after the class, as an appropriate occasion arises. Do not be shy or afraid that the teacher or your classmates will think you are ignorant for asking a silly question. If you have a question, then raise it; and if you have nothing to say, then remain silent. If you have done your reading ahead of time, you will be able to answer many of the questions raised in class by your instructor. This will give the impression that you are mentally sharp and well-prepared.

It is important to remember that reading assignments are a means to an end, rather than an end in itself. If you did not fully understand your reading assignment the first time, then you can read it again if you have time. But this should be done *before* you attend the class in which the material will be discussed. Do not go back and read the material after class, because you will only find yourself falling behind. You will not even need to re-read the material before a test, because it was only a means to help you better understand the lecture—which is what the test will be based on.

I have seen many students make an absolute fetish out of the reading assignments. They underline different passages in their textbooks using various shades of magic marker, which they read and re-read several times in preparation for a test. The ones who are most likely to use this approach are those who do not attend lectures regularly or who take only sparse notes when they do attend class. Although this approach may look like an organized system, it is a big waste of time. The instructor does not care how much of the reading material you can memorize by rote, but, rather, how well you have mastered the material presented in class.

I have one final caution to students who are trying to find a short-cut around their reading assignments. Don't assume that you will not have to do the readings because all of the exam questions will be based on the lecture. You have to do the readings in order to fully understand the lecture. Besides, there is more to a course than the material covered in the lecture. Your instructor will not have time to discuss everything about the course during the lecture, only the most significant aspects. The readings often include interesting material not covered in class which you should know if you are to master the subject. Obtain a good return on your investment in school by always doing all of the reading assignments. An old Italian proverb is very appropriate here: "The longest way round is the shortest way home."

Although written homework assignments are rare in some college subjects, it is not uncommon to receive a written homework assignment after every lecture in mathematics and the sciences. This is in the nature of these disciplines, since you master the material by doing, and you cannot go forward to the next step until you master the previous one. Simply watching the instructor work problems in class will not teach you all of the nuances of problem solving. This is similar to what George Bernard Shaw meant when he said, "If you teach a man anything, he will never learn." You have to roll up your sleeves, use your head, get your hands a little dirty, and make some mistakes to really learn the material. Your objective should be to make the mistakes and learn the proper methods before the exam.

Some instructors who are very conscientious collect homework assignments, grade them, and return them to the student. It is imperative that you complete these assignments on time, both to send the proper signal to the instructor and to enable yourself to progress at the proper pace. If you do not complete these homework assignments on schedule, you will quickly find yourself falling behind and recovery will become increasingly difficult. It is always wise to turn in all of the homework assigned for a course, even if it is late.

You should not think of homework assignments as punishment meted out by your instructor but, rather, as a device for helping you to become more knowledgeable about the subject matter. Correspondingly, you should approach them in earnest and with enthusiasm. As Ralph Waldo Emerson said, "Nothing great was ever achieved without enthusiasm." If you do not understand some of the homework questions, you should ask the instructor for clarification. It is quite possible that questions similar to those given as homework may appear on an examination.

If you want to get the most from your classroom lecture, then follow—

PRINCIPLE 5
Complete your assignment before going to class.

6
TAKE EXTENSIVE NOTES DURING LECTURE

In *Henry IV*, William Shakespeare wrote, "It is the disease of not listening, the malady of not marking, that I am troubled withal." What was true in Shakespeare's day is still true today. You must listen carefully to your instructor during class and take extensive notes on the lecture if you have any hope of becoming a straight-A student.

This step is probably the most crucial part of my entire system. You must make an effort to capture everything of significance presented by your instructor, because you will be tested on material covered during class lectures. This will require you to use all of your listening ability and concentration during the lecture, and to have a good system for recording what was said. If you obtain little or nothing from your class lectures, then you should not expect to do very well in the course. The purpose of this chapter is to show you how to become an effective listener and note-taker.

Let's concentrate first on your listening ability. Do you know what distinguishes a good listener from a poor listener?

One of the salient traits of poor listeners is that they hear only what they want to hear. They may be suffering from any of a number of blocks to effective listening. Some of these blocks include not being interested in the course, dislike of the instructor, being easily distracted by noise in the classroom or the mannerisms of others, and lack of concentration. You must avoid these pitfalls if you are to become an effective listener.

The stage is already set for you to be a good listener if you are sitting in the front row and have read your assignment beforehand, but much more is required. You will have to learn how to be a good listener on your own, because the typical college curriculum does not contain courses that teach this skill.

Unlike reading, writing, or thinking—in which you have complete control—listening involves the presence of another person. In order to be a good listener, you have to be a good follower. You will need to focus your concentration on the lecturer's line of thought and avoid drifting off on tangents. This is more difficult than it sounds because you can think several times faster than your instructor can speak. You can use this extra time to think about what your instructor has said, record the statements in your notes, and anticipate the next thought. But do not spend too much time thinking "around the thought" or you will miss your instructor's next thought. If your instructor says something that intrigues you, avoid thinking about it deeply at that time. There is plenty of time after class to think deep thoughts. The best strategy is to temporarily accept what has been said and be a good follower.

Now I am not suggesting that you blindly follow your instructor like a God. Instructors do not know everything and they often make mistakes. As Seneca, the Roman philosopher, said, "Even while they teach, men learn." If your teacher says something that you do not understand, or that does not sound correct, then question it. Buy try to be intelligent about asking questions in class. Ask a question of your instructor if you really need assistance but don't be so impatient to ask the question that you interrupt the instructor or disrupt the class. Ask questions that are worthy of consideration rather than raising questions merely because you wish to be heard. As

Oliver Wendell Holmes, the American physician and author, once noted, "It is the province of knowledge to speak and it is the privilege of wisdom to listen."

Good listeners are very attentive during lectures, because they know that there is only one chance to grasp the material. This contrasts sharply with reading a book because you can read a passage several times until you comprehend it. You must always be attentive during a lecture or you run the risk of missing important material that will appear later on a test. One way to be attentive is to use all of your senses to gather information during the lecture. Your eyes should alternate between the blackboard and your notebook, your ears should be attuned to your lecturer's words, and your mind should be working on understanding and synthesizing the lecture. Your entire body should be working continuously to understand the nuance of every thought expressed in class. When you become this involved, you are less likely to drift off or be distracted.

The most effective way to become a good listener is to take good notes, and the way to take good notes is to be a good listener. In other words, taking good notes and becoming a good listener go hand-in-hand.

The first rule for effective note-taking is to bring the proper supplies to class to take notes. I recommend using standard-size spiral notebooks with pages that do not come out, so you will not lose anything or be reduced to a shambles should you drop your notebook. You may want to consider purchasing separate notebooks for every course, since you will be taking extensive notes. Always take your notes in pencil and have a good eraser available. It is very difficult to make changes to notes taken in ink, if you or the teacher have made a mistake that needs to be corrected. If you have to cross through a lot of text written in ink, your notes will look very sloppy and be difficult to read. Be sure to bring any other supplies to class that you know will be needed, such as rulers, compasses, and so forth.

The best way to mentally capture the material presented by the instructor in class is to take extensive notes during the lecture. You should attempt to write down every significant thought expressed by the teacher in class. Forget about trying to record informal discussion, jokes, or other trivial matters. Concentrate on recording what the teacher says rather than trying to translate it into your own words—that will come later. Otherwise, you may miss a significant thought or use words that express a thought incorrectly. Do not try to construct elaborate outlines during a lecture to organize the material, unless the instructor has provided one as part of the presentation. If the instructor draws graphs, charts and tables on the blackboard during a lecture, be sure to record them in your notes.

The usefulness of your notes for studying for an exam is only as good as the information that goes into them. My advice to you on taking notes is that given to me by a former English professor: "Be thou dull, be thou labored, but be thou accurate."

You cannot literally write every word spoken by the teacher unless you know shorthand and write very fast, so I have a somewhat different approach for you. I developed a standard set of abbreviations that made good sense to me, even though they may have looked like pidgin English to someone else. These abbreviations enabled me to write very fast and capture almost all of the substance presented by an instructor. I could then take this abbreviated text and translate it into very readable English, which is what you will need to do in the next step.

It is impossible in this short space for me to provide a detailed description of my system for abbreviating the English language. What I will do instead is to describe the major techniques I use for abbreviation and fast note-taking. Abbreviate common words by using the first few and last few letters in the word; leave out vowels and use contractions where possible. Try to use the same abbreviations for words so it will be easier to decipher them when rewriting your lecture notes. There are several abbreviations that can be used for standard phrases, such as: for example (e.g.), equals (=), does not equal ($\neq$), and (&), with (w/), and without (w/o). You do not need to write complete sentences; leave out conjunctions, prepositions, and other words which are not essential to understand the thought. You should be very careful, however, to avoid leaving out words which could change the meaning of the thought. The objective is to do as little writing as possible and still capture all of the facts, principles, and ideas expressed by the lecturer.

You will need a good system to organize all of these notes. Be sure to write down the date at the beginning of each lecture, and number the pages so you can keep track of what you are doing. Make a note of your assignments, what they involve, and when they are due.

As you take notes in class, you should be on the alert for potential exam questions. If you are very attentive, you may notice a change in your instructor's gestures or tone of voice when emphasizing a significant principle or idea. When a teacher becomes very excited about the material or stresses a particular point, there is a good chance that it will show up on an exam. Some teachers cannot conceal their emotions, and they telegraph their intentions very clearly. Other instructors are more outspoken and often remark in class that certain material would make a good question on an exam.

Professors hint, too, sometimes over and over again. So take the hint! Being able to spot a potential exam question puts you one step up on the other students because you have a chance to collect your thoughts and prepare an answer beforehand.

Different professors have different styles in presenting their lectures. Some provide an outline of material to be covered during class, others number their points or repeat them several times for emphasis, and still others hand out written summaries of the content of their lectures. Being able to recognize your instructor's style will help you to organize the material better and get more out of the lecture because you know what to expect.

I realize that I have laid out a very difficult task for some of you, because it will require you to listen and digest material more completely than you have ever experienced before. You will need to work harder in class, but you will soon adjust to the sore fingers from all of the writing as you get into a groove.

If you take extensive and complete notes as I have outlined in this section, you will find that you become more involved in the learning process. Your body and mind will be working almost every second that you are in class, digesting and synthesizing the material. When you become this involved, you will find that time passes very quickly, and you are less cognizant of the amount of work you are doing. In time, you will feel more exhilarated as you gain command over the material. The entire learning experience will become more enjoyable and you will look forward to the next class. You will learn to enjoy the feeling of being a few steps ahead of your classmates and, occasionally, the teacher.

I also have an important caution—don't look for an easy way out of hard work! You should not think that you can use a tape recorder instead of taking detailed notes in class. You are probably less likely to listen to your lecturer if the tape recorder is running, because you know you will be able to listen to it later. It is very hard to make much sense out of a tape recording when the teacher is referring to something on a blackboard that is no longer in front of you. Besides, your understanding and retention of the material is much better if you write it down immediately after you hear it.

Even if you can fully understand your instructor's lecture without taking notes, this does not absolve you of the need to take notes. There is no guarantee that you will remember the material at a later date. The only way to be certain is to take careful detailed notes. This will involve a lot of hard work but, as Thomas Edison said, "There is no substitute for hard work."

PRINCIPLE 6
Take extensive notes during lecture.

7

REWRITE YOUR LECTURE NOTES BEFORE THE NEXT CLASS

Euripides' statement that "In this world second thoughts, it seems, are best" is even more appropriate here. You should always review and rewrite your lecture notes a second time, before the next class.

I normally kept two different sets of notebooks for every class. I would use the first set to take my abbreviated notes in pencil during a lecture. I would then rewrite the notes in longhand and in ink into the second set before attending the next class. The permanent set of notes in ink never left my room. Since notes are a key element in the system, you simply cannot afford to lose them. By following this system, you will have a back-up set of notes should you lose the note book you normally carry to class.

Shortly after attending a lecture, pick a quiet spot where you can really concentrate on what you have written in class and rewrite your notes. As you rewrite your lecture notes you are re-thinking the material presented in class. You are translating your abbreviated set of notes into complete thoughts and sentences. As you do this, you are resolving any inconsistencies and incomplete thoughts raised during the lecture. During the rewriting phase, make sure that you can distinguish major points from minor details. It may be helpful to organize your notes in outline form.

I am not suggesting that you rearrange the lecture material during rewriting, but merely that you add headings that outline the overall framework of the lecture. It is also a good idea to add your own personal comments and criticisms into your rewritten notes, but with a clear indication that they are yours rather than the instructor's. They may be very helpful if you are asked to express an opinion on a topic during an exam.

Make sure that you really understand what you have written, rather than taking it for granted. Rewrite your notes in an active manner, inquiring about the meaning and importance of your teacher's statements and, in particular, their relevance for potential exam questions.

If your notes have inconsistencies that you cannot resolve on your own, then ask the teacher to resolve them for you either before or during the next class. You can visit your instructor during office hours if you need additional time to resolve a particular troublesome problem. This type of feedback not only ensures that you and the teacher are on the same wavelength, it sends an important signal to the teacher that you are a serious student who is actively engaged in the learning process.

The most effective way to master ideas is to rewrite them, because this forces you to re-think them in a very deliberate way. Your rewritten notes will be expressed in a manner that is most accessible to your mind. You will find it much easier to review your rewritten notes later on, because you will not have to re-learn the material.

The most important reason for rewriting your notes *before* the next class is that you have already started to study for the exam. You cannot begin studying for the exam too soon.

By rewriting your notes before the next class you will be reviewing the material when your grasp of it is strongest, because it is still fresh in your mind. If you waited a long time before rewriting, you would not be able to reconstruct what the instructor said to fill in the missing pieces. As you rewrite your notes, your mind becomes more familiar with the material and you begin to internalize it. Thoughts received in this manner have much greater residual power than when reviewed after a length of time. I have found that I can still remember much of the material I studied several years ago. This is an important quality. As an anonymous person once said, "Education is what you have left over after you have forgotten everything you have learned."

My recommendation to rewrite lecture notes may be controversial, but I feel that it is one of the most important aspects of my system of study. Most other study guides advise students very emphatically not to rewrite their lecture notes, referring to its as a superstitious, mindless activity. The typical approach recommended by these guides is to outline the teacher's presentation during a lecture, translating the teacher's thoughts into your own words. They advise the student to reread lecture notes shortly after class and supplement them as necessary. I have found it more effective to completely rewrite the teacher's thoughts—which were faithfully recorded in notes taken during class—into a separate set of lecture notes after class, with supplementation as necessary. All I can tell you is that I have tried it both ways, and my approach works best. As the acid test, you can compare my grades with those of authors who espouse the alternative viewpoint.

Potential controversy aside, it is very difficult to convince students of the importance of rewriting lecture notes. Although it is a very easy, straightforward task, many students will make a chore out of it. Many students view it as a time-consuming, laborious, and unnecessary activity. They may feel that writing their notes once is sufficient to master the material. In all likelihood, they will not look at their lecture notes until just before a test, only to be surprised that much of what they have written does not make any sense.

Don't be swayed by this faulty line of reasoning. Although it takes a little more time in the short run to rewrite lecture notes, it will actually take less time in the long run to review them in preparation for a test. Your retention will be greater and you already will have mastered the materials, so the review process will be much easier.

The proper approach is to allot your time carefully so that you are able to rewrite lecture notes for all of your classes before the next lecture, and complete your reading assignments as well. You will develop a system that will allow you to get everything done in time and still have time left over for leisure activities. But you cannot skimp on any of the steps of the system, because you will not be following the system. Rewriting lecture notes is essential!

I rest my case with the following facts. Experiments in information theory have shown that average persons retain only about 20 percent of what they read, 40 percent if they have heard it after they read it, and 60 percent if they also write it. Thus, even if you do all of the reading assignments, attend class regularly and listen carefully, and take good lecture notes, you will barely know enough to get a passing grade. By rewriting your lecture notes, you raise your retention level significantly above 60 percent.

The remaining steps in this section will show you how to increase your mastery of the material as close to the 100 percent mark as possible.

PRINCIPLE 7
*Rewrite your lecture notes before
the next class.*

8

START REVIEWING YOUR LECTURE NOTES ONE WEEK BEFORE A TEST

Robert Louis Stevenson once wrote, "Even if the doctor does not give you a year, even if he hesitates about a month, make one brave push and see what can be accomplished in a week." There is nothing magical about a one-week time period, but the point is that you have to start studying early to do well on an exam. A lot can be accomplished in just one week!

Actually, you have been studying for the exam much longer than a week if you have been rewriting your lecture notes throughout the semester. If you have followed the previous steps, you have mastered the material as it was presented to you. This does not mean, however, that you have full command over the material for a test. With the passage of time, the ideas and concepts that were once very clear in our minds begin to fade. Even though your memory may not have dissolved, the longer it has been since the last test the hazier your understanding of the material is likely to be. Therefore, you should thoroughly review your notes before you take a test.

Most instructors announce examinations well in advance in order to give you ample opportunity to study for them. In fact, most instructors announce their exam schedule at the beginning of the semester. This will allow you to plan your schedule very carefully. If your instructor has not provided information about the exam schedule then seek it out—repeatedly if necessary!

Some instructors like to preserve the element of surprise by giving unannounced quizzes to make sure that students are keeping up with their studies. Although I regard this as a dirty trick, you will be better prepared than your fellow students if you have been rewriting your notes throughout the semester.

To prepare for an exam, all you will have to do is review your rewritten lecture notes. As I noted earlier, you will not have to go back and review any of the reading assignments. Reviewing your lecture notes should be a painless experience, because you have rewritten them in a fashion that is easy to read and all inconsistencies have been resolved. The information is already ingrained in your mind, since you have rewritten the notes once. All you need to do is to review the material sufficiently so that you have control over it. When you get control over the material, you will have control over the situation.

You should start your review one week in advance of the test by reading through your notes at a leisurely pace. Why at a leisurely pace? As Samuel Johnson said, "All intellectual improvement arises from leisure." If you cannot cover all of the material in one sitting, then pick up where you left off the next day. Do not spend too much time during this first review by trying to master all of the interrelationships or commit everything in your notes to memory. This initial reading serves as a refresher, and builds your confidence that you have an understanding of the material that will be covered on the test. The next few phases of the review will give you complete mastery over the material.

The best way to master the material is to re-read your lecture notes several times. After you have finished your first review of the notes, you should have about five or six days left before the exam. Give yourself a short breather and start your second review. Approach the second review in a more active manner than the first. Make sure that you clearly distinguish major from minor topics and understand important definitions. Get command over the material by reciting details under major points. If you find that you are unable to retain details during this rehearsal, try to tie them in with other facts or relationships that you are already knowledgeable about. Relate the information to your own personal experiences if you can, because it will be easier to retain. Sometimes you can identify a few key words that will help trigger your memory about a whole body of knowledge.

You will find this second review to be considerably easier than the first. As you review the material a second time, you will start to anticipate the sequence of ideas, because the material is fresh in your mind from the first review. This review process will help you to internalize the material so that you can reproduce or manipulate it at will. You will become more comfortable as you master the material, and your confidence will start to soar.

After you have finished your second review, give yourself a short breather and then start your third review. By this time, you can almost anticipate the content of the next page, not just the sequence of ideas. More importantly, you will start to relate the material between different sections, which often is what is required on an examination. You will start to feel very confident about your mastery of the material and you will look forward to the examination so you can demonstrate your knowledge.

You can repeat this review process as many times as you want before the test, as time allows. The more times you conduct your review, the more complete your mastery of the material. In preparing for any test, a good general rule is never review your lecture notes fewer than *three* times or you may be in trouble. Now, don't become obsessive and feel that you have to review your notes ten times to build complete mastery. Besides, you will start to experience diminishing returns beyond some point because you have already gleaned most of the content.

The following anonymous poem was found in an old Elizabethan manuscript:

> *Multiplication is vexation,*
> *Division is as bad;*
> *The rule of three doth puzzle me,*
> *And practice drives me mad.*

Whether the rule of three puzzles you, or practice drives you mad, you are going to have to face up to the fact that you need to review your lecture notes several times to master the material. There is no other way to do it. I have a few additional pointers that will assist you in this effort.

Think about potential exam questions. It is impossible to guess all of the questions that will appear on an exam, since much of the obvious material is never tested. Nevertheless, it is still worth your while to try and anticipate probable exam questions. This should not be too difficult, since the material will likely group into certain major themes. It is easier to recognize these themes after several reviews of your notes. Ask yourself hypothetical questions and think about how you would answer them. Organize the material in your mind and think about the sequence of points that you would write on an exam. Recite the answer in your own words, either silently or out loud. Active rehearsal helps you to obtain a better grasp of the material and to retain it for a longer period of time. This will give you good experience in expressing yourself, which is what is required on examinations. It is a very good drill that will help you to prepare for the real exam.

Rewrite equations and graphs. Certain fields such as mathematics, economics, and chemistry rely heavily on symbols, equations, and graphs. Reviewing your lecture notes several times may not be sufficient to give you total command over the material. In such cases, you can augment your review by rewriting the equations and graphs until you feel completely at ease with them. You will find that you are able to reproduce mathematics symbols much more readily if you write them several times. This exercise is particularly useful for graphs because it will help you to remember the relationship of various lines and the proper labels for axes.

You can rewrite these expressions on a blackboard, a piece of paper, or anything you choose. The approach I used was to rewrite them directly into my finished set of lecture notes. I would write my permanent set of lecture notes on every other page, which left ample room for rewriting any expressions that I needed to practice. I could then compare my rewritten expressions with the lecture notes on the opposite facing page to make sure that everything was correct. This exercise will give you good practice for the examination. If you find that you are having a lot of trouble with particular mathematical expressions or graphs, then jot them down on a separate piece of paper so you can look at them periodically—right up to the day of the exam, if necessary.

Pay attention to materials distributed in class. Instructors will sometimes hand out additional reading materials if they do not have time to cover all of the information in class, or if the material is very involved. The mere fact that the teacher has handed this material out should impress its importance on you. As William James once said, "A thing is important if anyone *think* it important." You should treat this material as if it were actually presented in the lecture. This means that you should rewrite all of the material (as long as it is not too extensive), as you have been doing with your lecture notes. Be sure that you recognize the relationship between the material in the handout and the material presented in the classroom lecture. I can remember several instances where such material figured very prominently in examinations, so it is wise to be prepared.

In the unlikely event that the instructor announced that you will be tested on certain readings, you should also treat this material as if it were actually presented in the lecture. This does not mean that you should rewrite all of the readings, but you should make sure that you have mastered the material.

In most cases it will be sufficient to outline the relevant part of the readings and review the outline along with your lecture notes in preparation for a test.

If you have to memmorize, then memorize. In most college courses you will not have to memorize a lot of material; understanding is a far more important skill. In some courses, however, there will be key principles and definitions that you are expected to remember. In most cases, you can master these by rewriting your notes and locking them into your permanent memory while studying for an exam. If this is not sufficient, then you will have to do something extra to memorize the material. The problem is that most students do not know how to go about memorizing information. They stare at the words on a page for a lengthy period of time, hoping to absorb the information through a process similar to osmosis. This is a backward approach.

Here is a straightforward approach that will help you to memorize information more effectively. Record information that you need to remember on 3″ × 5″ index cards. Write the word or principle on the front of the card and its meaning and other pertinent information on the back of the card. In your spare moments, glance at the front of the card and see if you can remember what is on the back of the card. Repeat this as necessary until you master the material.

Conduct your review in an organized and continuous manner. Since you started your review at least one week before the test, you should have ample time to review and master the material. Try to continue your review throughout this week rather than allow several days to elapse between reviews. I know that this can be very difficult if you have a busy schedule in which you are taking several courses and participating in extra-curricular activities, but you just have to be diligent during this period. The continuity of study is important if you are to master the material. Continuity of study helps you to get control over the material very quickly because you do not have to go back and remember where you left off at your last reading. I tried to conduct my review of the lecture notes during every day of the week prior to an exam, except the day of the exam itself.

You will find that you can accomplish much more if you study for several hours at a time rather than conduct your review in several small time intervals. Long study periods are effective for understanding interrelationships between the various topics in a subject. This is the stuff that exams are made of. Some study guides advise you to "think small" and study in small time intervals. I disagree with this approach. My philosophy is to "think big"—both in terms of completing a lot of work and making the highest possible grades on exams.

Never study up to the last minute before an exam. If you have been studying very hard for a test, exercise a little moderation and stop the day before—or at least a few hours before—you take the exam. As Benjamin Disraeli said, "There is moderation even in excess." Studying up to the last minute is a disconcerting experience. It means that you have run out of time, because you did not start early enough to master the material. You will feel much more confident if you do not have to cram everything into your head in the final hours before the test. Besides, your mind needs some rest before the exam, because you will need all of your energy and ingenuity to do a first-rate job on the exam. The importance of rest cannot be over-emphasized. You have to be mentally sharp and relaxed to perform up to your potential on an examination.

You should not be concerned that you will forget a lot of information by the time of the test if you started your studying a week in advance. Retention of material tends to be quite good if you really understand ideas and their interrelationships rather than isolated bits of information. Your retention will be much better if you were able to tie your new knowledge in with some important aspect of your life. The goal of education is not only to increase your knowledge but to give you a lasting wisdom in dealing with the world. As Alfred, Lord Tennyson said, "Knowledge comes, but wisdom lingers."

I have one final point to make on studying. I know that some study guides recommend preparing for exams in study groups, if you can find knowledgeable people who are willing to do a reasonable share of the work. I have never used this approach and, quite frankly, I guess that I am too much of an individualist to even try it. I feel that I can master the material on my own or get help from the instructor if necessary. To me, studying is a solitary endeavor, not a social affair. One thing is for certain: taking exams is a solitary activity because your friends will not be there to hold your hand or tell you the answers; if they are, it is called cheating.

Remember, if you want to do well on exams you have to study for them. Don't think for a minute that you might get lucky and do well on an exam without studying. If you go into an exam with an empty head, don't expect your score to be much better. As Benjamin Franklin said, "An empty bag cannot stand upright." How high the bag gets filled, and how upright you stand, depends on how much you study. Follow—

PRINCIPLE 8
Start reviewing your lecture notes one week before a test.

9

BE TEST-WISE AND TAKE YOUR EXAM IN COMPLETE CONFIDENCE

There is a verse in the English Prayer Book which reads, "Examine me, O Lord, and prove me: try out my reins and my heart." Even though you will be going before a much lesser authority on an exam, the need to be prepared is still present. Your instructor may not try out your reins and your heart, but you can be sure that he or she will try out your mind.

The first and foremost principle in taking tests is that you need to know what you are doing—to be test-wise. Chapter 2 of Part Two was concerned with the basic skills of test-taking. That chapter covered the general strategies for taking tests, as well as the specific strategies for taking various types of tests. The present chapter presumes that you are now a test-wise student, and moves on to some of the more esoteric aspects of test-taking. If you have not mastered the material in Chapter 2 of Part Two, which is likely with one reading, then you should review it at some point. If you read Chapter 2 in haste, then re-read it at your leisure.

If you have followed the first eight steps of my system, you should have complete mastery over the material. Your task now is to demonstrate this mastery to the instructor. If the instructor asks for a recitation of material, then your task is very straightforward. If you have a good instructor, however, it is unlikely that you will be asked to regurgitate the material verbatim on an exam. The most effective tests ask you to use the information at your command to solve a problem that is new. This may require the combination of information in ways that were not discussed by the instructor. This is similar to the way you will have to approach problems in the real world, because they typically do not fall into neat textbook cases. New ideas are always difficult to handle, whether they are encountered inside or outside the classroom.

Instructors are particularly fond of asking you to apply methods taught in class to solve a new problem. These methods are like a bag of tools available to a skilled craftsman. You have to know what tools to use on a particular problem and how to use them. Tools are very important in certain courses, such as the physical and social sciences. For example, mathematical equations and graphical analyses are indispensable tools to the economist. Other disciplines require different sets of tools. In an examination, you need to be able to demonstrate to the instructor that you know how to use the tools of the trade like a journeyman.

You should go into a test with a completely open mind. When taking a test, you should not try to force your answers exactly into the mold that fits your notes. The teacher may be asking you to apply your knowledge in a different way. Sometimes you need to move out of your ordinary way of thinking and be creative to come up with a good answer. If you have vigorously studied your lecture notes during the week prior to the exam, you have bombarded your mind with a wide assortment of information. Your mind will be working with this information on a subconscious level, exploring the interrelationships between various facts, principles, and ideas. This prior preparation should put you in a creative mood for the test.

In order to reach the full potential of your creativity, you should go into an exam with the proper mental attitude and a high degree of self-confidence. You should think of an exam as an opportunity to show the instructor how much you have learned. If you have been following my system, you will be able to take your exam in tranquility because your mind will be well ordered. If you are confident, you are more likely to do well because you have the proper mental attitude. If your confidence is low, you are bound to do poorly. It is a self-fullfilling prophecy.

We have all heard athletic coaches talk about the importance of confidence when competing in sports. Mental confidence helps an athlete to perform at the highest level and gain an advantage over the competitors. Taking an exam is similar to an athletic event, because you are competing against the instructor and other persons in the class. You are also competing against yourself, in a certain sense, because you will be trying to approach perfection in composing your answer. As in an athletic competition, you should aim your sights high and be confident that you can reach the pinnacle.

At the opposite end of the spectrum of human emotions is fear. Many people experience fear and anxiety at the thought of having to take an exam. They become nervous, worrisome, and even ill about exams because they have a fear of failure. They fantasize about the catastrophic repercussions and misfortunes that will befall them if they do poorly on an exam. They worry about the criticism and ridicule that will come from relatives, teachers, and peers. Some people become very anxious about taking exams because they feel that the stakes are very high. Persons who have spent an excessive amount of time studying for an exam may feel that they must get a high grade to justify their efforts. The very thought that they will not do well can result in nervousness and anxiety. They become so worried about taking a test that their reasoning and thinking ability is impaired and they actually bring about the very thing they hoped to avoid.

You should not confuse the fear of failure with the desire for success. It is entirely natural to become "psyched-up" for an examination in anticipation of what is to come. A little emotion and a healthy flow of adrenaline can heighten your senses and sharpen your mental acuity, improving your performance on the test. This is a very different reaction, indeed, from fear.

Most of the fears and insecurities experienced by students before a test are due to a lack of self-confidence. Students who have scored poorly on exams in the past or who have no confidence in their preparation for a test are the ones most likely to fall into this syndrome. You can be confident that you will do well on exams if you have been following my study methods. As you experience more success on exams, your fears should dissipate because you will know that you have done everything possible to realize your potential.

How does one go about getting rid of fear? If you have experienced fear associated with taking tests, you may find it somewhat difficult to change your attitude immediately. You may find it easier to cope with fear if you have a better understanding of what tests are all about. An examination gives you a quantitative assessment of your knowledge on a subject and indicates where improvement is needed. It is important to recognize that examinations are not an assessment of the intrinsic worth of an individual, but merely an assessment of how much he or she knows about a particular subject. Examinations are less threatening when thought of in this manner. You should never lower your self-esteem because you have performed poorly on a test.

Tests are essentially a learning device, providing you and your teacher with valuable information to evaluate your performance and progress. You should recognize that no one is perfect—all humans are bound to make mistakes. Your goal should be to make your mistakes before the exam, learn from them, and avoid repeating them on the exam. Unfortunately, it is not always so easy to do this. As the philosopher Soren Kierkegaard said, "Life can only be understood backwards; but it must be lived forwards."

Most instructors review the correct answers to the questions when they return the examination. If you have made mistakes on the exam, you should learn where you went wrong so you will not repeat them in the next test, the final, the next course, or, for that matter, life. If you can learn from your mistakes, the stage is set for further growth.

Tests also enable you to learn something about your instructor. Although teachers do not usually ask the same questions on tests from semester to semester, they exhibit a certain style in the type and scope of questions asked. You should attempt to understand your teacher's M.O. (modus operandi), just as a master detective studies the behavior patterns of criminals to anticipate their next move. (Teachers, please excuse the analogy.) After you take your first test from an instructor, you should analyze the situation. Did the teacher give an essay or objective exam, or some other type of test? What kinds of questions were asked? Was the emphasis on memorizing facts, understanding ideas and their interrelationships, or applying principles? Was the teacher looking for major themes or mastery of minutiae? Sizing up the teacher's M.O. can help you prepare for the next exam and the final.

You can also obtain a better perspective about exams if you understand how they are graded. Most instructors award grades in a distribution approximating the normal distribution in statistics. In other words, only a few students will be given the highest grades, most will be located in the broad middle-range, and only a few will fail. As Gore Vidal, the American novelist, said, "It is not enough to succeed. Others must fail." Many teachers like to grade according to the normal curve because they feel it is objective. But their real reason may be that it is more convenient than setting up their own more reasonable standards. Occasionally you will encounter an instructor who announces that everyone can get an A or everyone can get an F, but this is rare. The university administration will not allow an instructor to maintain such a position for very long. Normally you will have to compete vigorously for one of the few A's that will be awarded.

When you are graded on a curve, your grade is just as much a reflection of how smart your classmates are as how much you have learned in the course. If there are a number of good students in your class, the competition will likely be very keen. On the other hand, if there are a number of poor students, they help to pad out the lower end of the grading curve. You should be thankful for their presence.

You should recognize that grading essay exams is a very subjective and fickle affair. The grade you receive is probably a function of what other students graded before you have received, particularly if grades are awarded according to a curve. Your grade will also be a function of the particular qualities your instructor holds dear, such an understanding of ideas, organization and presentation of the argument, grammar, spelling, handwriting, how well he or she thinks you understand the material based on your classroom participation, and probably a number of other factors. The important consideration is what your instructor thinks is important. It is often difficult to figure this out in advance. As you become more familiar with your instructor, you will know what to emphasize on tests.

Some of the problems students have with exams can be avoided if they concentrate on mastering the subject rather than going for the grade. Actually, the two usually go hand-in-hand. It is possible that you know the subject but things just did not go right for you on the exam. If your emphasis is on mastering the subject and you have made your best effort possible, then you will derive some satisfaction even if your grade is not as high as you had hoped. There will always be other opportunities to demonstrate your knowledge.

I am not suggesting that you should be satisfied with suboptimal grades but, rather, that it may take you some time to reach the top. In the long run, your ultimate goal should be to become a straight-A student.

John Lyly, the English author, once said, "Let me stand to the main chance." An examination is your main chance to show the instructor what you know. Stand to it!

PRINCIPLE 9
Be test-wise and take your exam in complete confidence.

10

SHOW THE INSTRUCTOR WHAT YOU HAVE LEARNED ON THE FINAL

Demosthenes, the Athenian statesman, said, "Every advantage in the past is judged in the light of the final issue." Every advantage—and disadvantage—over the entire semester will be judged in light of your performance on the final exam. The final exam grade has a disproportionate effect on your final grade because it is the last exam grade given. Some instructors will give the student a final grade equal to the grade received on the final exam, regardless of past performance. It is somewhat similiar to the Christian ethic—you can repent at the last moment and redeem yourself.

The first thing that you need to do is to discover exactly what material will be covered on the final. Most instructors are very candid about the material that they will hold you responsible for on an exam. You should specifically ask the instructor whether the final will cover material presented throughout the entire semester or only since the last exam. The answer to this question will determine how you should go about studying for the final. If the final will cover only material since the last exam, then you should approach it like any other exam; in other words, re-read your lecture notes since the last exam several times. If the final will cover the entire course, you will need to go back and re-read your notes from the first lecture. This should not be too difficult because you are already very familiar with the earlier material.

Regardless of the scope of the final, you will be facing a very heavy workload at the end of the semester. The final examination period is very special because you are finishing up the semester and most of the exams are given around the same time. About one month before finals, take a close look at your schedule and determine exactly when each of your finals will occur. Work your way back from this point to determine how much time you will need to adequately prepare for each exam. If your schedule is bunched, you may need to start studying several weeks in advance rather than the customary one week period used throughout the semester.

You should approach your review of the material for finals in a slightly different manner than for regular exams. As a general rule, exams given during the semester test your knowledge on very specific topics. On the other hand, questions on finals typically inquire about major themes running through various topics presented throughout the semester. Look for these major themes as you review your entire set of lecture notes. This should be a relatively easy task if you have been following my methods, because you have mastered and retained the material presented earlier in the semester. After you have identified the major themes, make sure that you have knowledge of the specific details associated with these themes.

As part of your preparation for finals, you should review exams given earlier during the semester. Although it is unlikely that the same questions will appear on the final, you may see a pattern in the type of questions asked by your instructor. Make sure that you understand the complete answer to all questions asked on previous exams, particularly if you missed part or all of a question. Most instructors review exams when they return them to the student, and indicate what was expected for a good answer. You should have been taking notes on this review just as conscientiously as during a regular lecture. Your major objective should be to go into the final with a complete mastery of everything presented during the semester and to avoid making previous mistakes.

If you have time, you should also make an effort to look at final exams your instructor has given in previous semesters. Some instructors keep a file of past exams and make them available through the department or library. Other students or fraternal organizations occasionally retain exams. Your objective should be to get a feel for the types of questions the instructor asks on final exams. By the end of the semester, you should already have a good feel for the instructor's M.O. on regular exams, but he or she may choose to do something different on the final. By looking at previous finals, you will get a feeling for the number of questions asked and their nature and scope. Do not waste your time writing a complete answer to questions asked before, because it is unlikely that they will be asked again.

Your mental frame of mind during finals week will be an important determinant of your performance. You should approach your exams with a tranquil mind. If you have allowed yourself enough time for study, you will take your exams in a confident and relaxed manner. If, like most students, you have not allowed yourself enough time, the whole experience will be similar to a fraternal hell week.

Be very conscious about how you use your time to study, because it will slip away very quickly if you are not vigilant. Do not allow yourself to dwell on the fact that the final is the most important exam of the semester and everything is on the line. Follow the methods of study presented here, be confident and self-assured, and everything else will fall into line!

PRINCIPLE 10
*Show the instructor what you have
learned on the final.*

SUMMARY

**PART THREE
A SYSTEM FOR GETTING
STRAIGHT A'S**

PRINCIPLE 1
Plan a course of study.

PRINCIPLE 2
Choose your instructor.

PRINCIPLE 3
Never miss a class.

PRINCIPLE 4
Always sit in the front row.

PRINCIPLE 5
*Complete your reading assignment
before going to class.*

PRINCIPLE 6
*Take extensive notes during
lecture.*

PRINCIPLE 7
*Rewrite your lecture notes before
the next class.*

PRINCIPLE 8
*Start reviewing your lecture notes
one week before a test.*

PRINCIPLE 9
*Be test-wise and take your exam in
complete confidence.*

PRINCIPLE 10
*Show your instructor what you have
learned on the final.*

PART FOUR

Making the System Work for You

1
STUDY TIPS

It is not enough to know how to do something, you must practice the proper behavior to accomplish your goals. If you are to become a straight-A student, you must know which study habits to practice and which to avoid.

Can you distinguish the good study habits from the bad ones, and do you know the basic principles for effective studying? The answer is really quite simple. As Rudyard Kipling wrote in the poem, *The Elephant's Child:*

> *I keep six honest serving men*
> *(They taught me all I knew);*
> *Their names are What and Why and When*
> *And How and Where and Who.*

You don't need to ask two of the serving men "Who" will be studying (You!) and "Why" it is important to study (if you read the chapter, "The Importance of Your Education"). Let's hear what the other four serving men have to say about the proper methods of study.

When to study. If you want to get better at your studies, then you should make an effort to study every day. This does

155

not mean that you should study continuously every day, or even study the same amount each day. But you should attempt to accomplish at least something every day in order to realize progress.

Some study guides advocate filling out elaborate calendars so you will know what you are supposed to be doing during every minute, hour, and day throughout the entire semester. They would have you allocate the time periods to study each subject, to eat meals, to engage in athletic events, to socialize with friends, and so forth. I feel that this approach is a serious mistake. Not only will students be unwilling to follow such schedules, it is undesirable for humans to attempt such regimentation. Following such a schedule would lead you to feel that your whole life is predetermined and you would quickly become bored with your studies. As Frederick Nietzsche, the German philosopher, inquired, "Is not life a hundred times too short for us to bore ourselves?" Use calendars for their intended purpose to record *significant* dates. Write down the dates of important events, such as exams and deadlines for term papers, so you will know how much time you have to prepare for them. Don't let calendars regulate your life!

Your planning horizon for studying should encompass only a few days at a time. Since most courses meet a couple of times a week, this will give you enough time to get ready for the next class. You now have a basic understanding of the work that is required. You need to read your assignment for the next class, rewrite your lecture notes, prepare for an exam (if one is coming up in the next week), spend some time working on a term paper (if you have one), or work on other assignments. The objective is to allocate your work over a few days at a time to accomplish these tasks for all of your courses, and still have time left over for other activities. Planning for only a few days at a time gives you the flexibility to make the frequent changes in schedule that are required for a very efficient use of time.

In order to make the best use of time, try to do your school work during periods when there are no competing activities that you want to participate in. For example, you can probably catch up on your reading assignments or rewriting your notes between classes when you would normally be wasting time. Or what about the time between when you wake up and when you start your first class? Or the time after class before the athletic event that you want to participate in starts? If you use these small time intervals efficiently, you can accomplish a lot.

How you budget your time will largely be a function of the hours that you want to keep open for leisure. For some individuals this will be during the day, and for others during the evening. Just make sure that you allow some time for leisure or you could burn yourself out. Use leisure time as a reward for getting your work done, which will give you an added incentive to study.

Where to Study. As written in the Book of Job in the Bible, "But where shall wisdom be found? and where is the place of understanding?" Your "place of understanding" for studying can be anywhere you choose, as long as it affords comfort and an opportunity to accomplish a significant amount of work. Some students find that they can study best in a particular chair or room. They associate this particular place with studying, and are able to work diligently and block out distractions when in that spot. Other students find that they can study best in the library, because of its atmosphere for learning. There is no single place of study that is best for all individuals.

The most important factor is to select a place of study where you can concentrate deeply for an extended period. Many students have problems with their concentration and often become fatigued after a few hours of study. However, some students can concentrate on their studies whether they are in noisy or quiet surroundings. Most people can adjust to the noise level in a room if they are deeply involved in their studies, but it is more disconcerting if the room changes alternatively from quiet to noisy, or vice versa. Many persons are more distracted by their internal frame of mind rather than by external phenomena. For example, we tend to become very distracted if we hear someone talking in the library, even if in a low voice, because we know that it is improper to do so. Or you may be distracted by your roommate, who is playing a song you do not like or tapping his or her fingers on a desk while studying. With a little forethought and some practice, we can avoid being distracted by such occurrences.

You should also recognize that there are "places of understanding" other than your formal study area. As I noted earlier, you will often find yourself reviewing the concepts you have studied, even during everyday activities such as getting dressed, eating meals, walking to class, and so forth. Another opportunity to practice new skills or illustrate new knowledge is during conversation with your friends and professors after class. I can remember getting together with a group of friends at a local college restaurant and having interesting intellectual discussions. This is particularly stimulating when you get an inter-disciplinary group together, because you can discuss several different dimensions of an issue.

What to Study. As mentioned earlier, you already have a basic understanding of what to study—you have to read assignments and rewrite lecture notes before the next class, and perhaps study for an exam or work on a paper as well. Let's get a little more specific on what to study.

When you sit down to do your studies, think about what you want to accomplish that day. Which subjects will you study and in what order? How many pages or chapters do you plan to read from your history book, how many mathematics problems will you attempt to solve, how much of your English theme will you attempt to write, and so forth? Challenge yourself to meet or exceed the goal you have set. If you work hard each day, you will see real progress and experience a sense of accomplishment.

I find that it is easier to think about how much I want to accomplish rather than how long I will study. Thinking about how much time you will spend on each subject can be distracting, because you may end up watching the clock. Do not set overly ambitious goals that are impossible to achieve, because this will only lead to frustration.

Samuel Johnson once said, "The great source of pleasure is variety." Alternate the order of the subjects you are studying to add some variety to your work. After doing something very quantitative like mathematics you may want to read a novel from your English course or a chapter from your history book. You can also alternate your studies between courses you find interesting and those you find tedious. If you hate chemistry but love English literature, reward yourself by reading a novel after doing your laboratory assignment. You will find that these substitutions enable you to relax and study for longer periods of time without becoming bored or taking excessive breaks. As noted by Anatole France, the French novelist, "Man is so made that he can only find relaxation from one kind of labor by taking up another."

You should never neglect studying for some of your courses, even if you feel that they are boring or tedious. Your objective should be to make an A in all of your courses, not solely in the ones you enjoy. If you neglect doing your work in a boring course, you may fall so far behind that you are never able to recuperate. If you neglect doing your work in a course long enough, the whole course will be lost!

How to Study. William James once said, "There is no more miserable human being than one in whom nothing is habitual but indecision." Before you sit down to study, decide whether you really want to be studying at that time or doing something else. If you have something else to do—something worthwhile—then postpone studying until a later time. However, you should never procrastinate in your studies merely because you dislike a course or feel lazy. You will have to do the work at a later time anyway, leaving less time to do other things that you find more desirable. You must always maintain the self-discipline to sit down and do the work that is required of you, like it or not.

When you finally sit down to study, "throw yourself" into your studies completely and do not let anything else interfere with your thought processes. You should approach your studies with enthusiasm, sincerity, and determination. To make the most efficient use of time, you should be able to sit down and start directly with your studies. If you are having a hard time getting into your studies, then start with some relatively easy aspect so you can ease into it gradually. You may occasionally be hesitant to start studying a subject because it looks difficult, but once you get into it you find that it is easier than you thought.

Always concentrate on accomplishing one thing at a time, to the exclusion of everything else. Maintain your concentration on what you are reading and don't try to watch television or converse with your friends at the same time. You cannot efficiently accomplish two separate activities simultaneously.

You will find that you can accomplish more if you work continuously over an extended period of time. I found that I could complete an enormous amount of work on the weekends, because I could work continuously without interruption. When you work continuously, you will not have to go back and review where you were at your last sitting. Moreover, your use of time will be more productive because you will be able to see the interrelationships between ideas more clearly. You will be amazed at how much you can accomplish if you stick with your studies for a couple of hours at each session. However, do not study for such a long period of time that the whole experience becomes gruelling or boring, because this will be counterproductive.

If you are studying for a long period of time, always allow time for periodic breaks. These breaks will provide a change of pace in what you are doing or serve as a transition to study a new subject. Always take at least a five- or ten-minute break each hour, but schedule them so the activity does not become indiscriminate and excessive. You can use the time between study periods to accomplish some chores, such as doing the laundry, cleaning your room, preparing meals, and so forth. This will give you a short mental break, while also accomplishing some work, so you can come back and hit your studies even harder. If the break is very short, you may want to just relax and do nothing. The need to goof-off occasionally is just as fundamental as the need for other necessities in life.

If you have been studying hard all day, take some time to wind down from your studies in the evening. Don't go directly from studying your assignments to bed, or you will feel like you are on a treadmill. Take a little time to do routine activities like brushing your teeth, getting your school materials ready for the next day, conversing with a friend, and so on. If you go directly to bed, the odds are that you will lie there for a half-hour or so with your head spinning like a top.

Practice good habits. You can increase the likelihood of doing well in school by following a few simple health rules. Always get plenty of rest, because you cannot think deeply or concentrate for any period of time if you are tired. Always eat three complete meals a day, because your energy level will be low if you are undernourished. I know that it can be difficult trying to get a nutritious diet on some of the food served in school cafeterias, but you should at least make an effort to stay away from junk foods—they will only make you sluggish. Like a trained athlete, you need to be at the top of your form to compete.

Regular exercise will help you to work harder and think more clearly. You will need some kind of release after spending so much time on your studies in a sedentary position. I find that a combination of walking, bicycling, and tennis keeps me fit both mentally and physically, and provides me with an opportunity to reflect on what I am doing and where I am going. Your preference may be jogging, swimming, or organized sports. Whatever your choice, keep active physically and you will perform better mentally.

Avoid bad habits. You will find it easier to practice good habits if you know to avoid bad habits. As Henry David Thoreau said, "A man is rich in proportion to the number of things which he can afford to let alone." Avoid activities that waste an excessive amount of time. A good example is television. You can waste huge amounts of time by sitting in front of the television set watching shows that you are not really interested in. Watching television is a compulsive habit that gives superficial satisfaction by portraying the experiences of others in contrived situations. With a high-quality education, you will have a greater opportunity to enjoy real-life experiences. Be selective and watch only the shows that you really want to see. Other classic time-wasters are shooting the bull with your friends and playing cards. These activities may be fun when you are engaged in them, but what do you have when you are finished? Less time to study and little else!

If you find that you do not have enough discipline to drop out of these activities after you have gotten into them, then it may be better to stay out of them altogether. As Mark Twain once said, "It is easier to stay out than get out."

We often find it difficult to accomplish everything we would like because we are not very efficient in our use of time. As a first step toward becoming more efficient, take a close look at how you are spending your time during a typical school week. What are the times when you are most and least likely to be productive? What are the times that were wasted altogether? Keeping track of time makes it much easier to pinpoint inefficiencies. If you are honest with yourself, you will probably be able to identify a number of occasions when you were not making the best use of time.

If you have not had good study habits in the past, then you may need to make some basic changes in your lifestyle. I realize that it is not so easy to change one's lifestyle overnight, since habits become very ingrained. Mark Twain also said, "Habit is habit, and not to be flung out the window by any man, but coaxed downstairs a step at a time." You should at least start to coax your bad habits downstairs today rather than wait until tomorrow. Regulate your life today and you won't have to worry about tomorrow.

It is just as much a bad habit to study too much as to study too little. Never become so fanatical and obsessed with your studies that you neglect your physical and mental well-being. We have all known or seen individuals on college campuses who are "spaced-out," as if they were suddenly dropped to earth from another planet or universe. We have all seen the "dirt-balls" who brush their teeth or comb their hair once a month (if that often) and who seem to be wearing clothes borrowed from a younger sibling. Some are so wrapped up in their studies that they have forgotten that they were once part of the human race—and they are not necessarily the ones who make the highest grades. This type of behavior is not only anti-social, it is counterproductive.

Yes, you can study too much. Your goal should be to study enough to make an A in all of your courses and then pursue leisure activities with the remaining time.

Henry David Thoreau once said, "I love a broad margin to my life." We all love a broad margin to our life, but most do not know how to obtain it because they have poor study habits. How many times have you pursued leisure activites, only to be plagued by guilt feelings because you feel that you should be studying instead. These ambivalent feelings arise because students lack confidence in their abilities or do not know how much study is required to do well. If you are practicing my system, you should not have these feelings, because you will know that you have done everything necessary to score top grades. You can throw yourself into leisure and other activities with more enthusiasm, because you will not be plagued by these conflicts. Even if you find that you do not have a broad margin to your life during an exam period, you will be able to enjoy the free time that you do have because you will not have to worry about your studies.

Adults returning to school will find that they have to be even more attentive about study habits than their younger classmates. The adult student may have forgotten much of the material learned years ago, the material itself may have changed, and study methods have probably long been forgotten. To make matters worse, the adult student is thrown into direct competition with younger students who are quick-witted, familiar with the latest material, and seem to have an unlimited amount of time to study. This last factor is a crucial difference. The adult student typically has many other responsibilities, as a parent, spouse, homeowner, worker, and so forth. There is barely enough time to complete all of life's little chores, much less find enough time to go to school and study for exams. The study methods presented here will be particularly useful to the adult student, because they show not only how to study to make top grades, but how to do it in minimum time. For additional study tips for the adult student, I recommend a fine book by Jerold Apps, *Study Skills for Adults Returning to School*, listed in my References.

John Ruskin, the English author, said, "In order that people may be happy in their work, these three things are needed: They must be fit for it. They must not do too much of it. And they must have a sense of success in it." Develop the proper study habits, and you will meet all three requirements.

PRINCIPLE 1
Develop the proper study habits and practice them continually if you want to become a straight-A student.

2
CONCLUSION

I have covered everything I know about how to become a straight-A student. I have reviewed the successes of other individuals who have made it and discussed the importance of obtaining a high-quality education. I have shown you how to improve your abilities in the basic skills, such as reading books, taking tests, and writing term papers. And I have presented a comprehensive system that begins with how to plan your studies, and shows you how to get the most from your classes, how to prepare assignments, how to study for tests, and how to make A's on tests. Moreover, I have suggested several study tips that will help you to conduct your studies in a timely and efficient manner and maintain your performance throughout your college career.

With a knowledge of this material, can you now expect to become a straight-A student? No, it is not that easy—much more is required!

The most important thing that you will need to do to make the system work for you is to actually follow it. You are not going to get straight A's merely because you have read this book and fully understood it. You have to practice each of the steps I have outlined, not just occasionally, but throughout the entire semester. If you do anything less, then you are not really following the system and you will not get the best results. I know this from past experience, and from the experience of others who have tried my methods. Few have the discipline and willpower to follow my system completely. Those who have been able to stick with the system have realized the greatest gains while those who have approached it casually have noticed little or no improvement.

Not only will you have to follow the system, you will have to work very, very hard. I can show you how to realize your potential, but I cannot wave a magic wand to relieve you of the workload. Hard work is the only road to success. Adopt the philosophy of President Theodore Roosevelt, who said, "I wish to preach, not the doctrine of ignoble ease, but the doctrine of the strenuous life."

Even the world's greatest geniuses have had to work very hard to achieve their fame. Don't take my word for it, take theirs. In his autobiography, *Life*, Thomas Edison said, "Genius is one percent inspiration and ninety-nine percent perspiration." Horace, the legendary Roman poet, said, "Life grants nothing to us mortals without hard work   And Michelangelo, the great Italian artist, said, "If people only knew how hard I work to gain my mastery, it wouldn't seem so wonderful at all."

What will it take for you to be willing to work this hard? You will have to approach your studies with passion and become highly motivated. Being motivated implies that you are interested in what you are doing, recognize its importance, and have the ambition and inspiration to work hard to achieve your goals. Motivation is the continual striving for excellence, the unwillingness to accept anything less than the very best, and the tenacity to keep trying no matter how difficult the situation.

As you increase your knowledge through study, you will become more motivated. As noted by Laurence Sterne, the British novelist, "The desire of knowledge, like the thirst of riches, increases ever with the acquisition of it."

Students often have difficulty getting motivated because they think they would prefer doing something else besides going to school. They long to get away from attending class and studying to go out in the working world where they can make some money. And when they get out into the working world they find that it is not always so pleasant. Working sometimes turns out to be an even bigger grind than school. As C.S. Lewis, the British novelist, once described life: "Term, holidays, term, holidays, till we leave school, and then work, work, work till we die." At least you have more free time while in school.

Think of the situation in the following way. Since you are going to be in school for a certain amount of time anyway, you might as well resolve yourself to work hard and make it a high-quality effort.

It is important to put forth your best effort at an early age, while there is still enough time to get into a good occupation that will bring greater financial rewards later on. Some employers are less willing to hire older workers, because they perceive them to be less adaptable. Many people work harder and become more productive as they mature, but their efforts sometimes come a little too late. Without the proper education, you may end up in a low-skilled, boring occupation that will break your back, your spirit, and your pocketbook.

If you are having difficulty getting motivated, then I have some advice for you. At times when you start wondering whether it is worth all the effort, take out the sheet of paper that contains your goals. Remind yourself of what you are trying to accomplish. Recognize that you are making an investment in the future, because how well you do in school will have an important influence on your station in life. If mastery of your studies increases your productivity, then you and society as a whole realize a benefit. You receive a personal benefit in the form of higher earnings, and society receives a benefit from a more educated populace and a higher level of economic well-being. As John Stuart Mill, the English economist, said, "The worth of a state, in the long run, is the worth of the individuals composing it." When you look at the "big picture," and your position in it, it is sometimes easier to get motivated to work hard.

Even if you are working very hard, you should recognize that you cannot accomplish everything at once. You should not be distraught if you do not achieve straight A's immediately. Having the proper knowledge is important, but we become most proficient at an activity through extensive practice. You should notice some improvement in your grades as soon as you start practicing my study methods, but it may take some time to perfect them. You should experience satisfaction as you move closer to that goal, recognizing that it often takes time to develop your study habits and attain your goals. As President Theodore Roosevelt recognized, "What I am to be, I am now becoming." Concentrate on what you need to do to become a straight-A student, rather than expecting to become one immediately.

You will occasionally need to push yourself to the limit in college. Although I received an A on every test in every course I took in graduate school, I can remember times when the going got a little rough. Sometimes things can get so rough that you feel you are in the middle of a war. Everything will be happening at once—term papers are due, tests are given back to back, and so forth. At these times, you have to keep a strong frame of mind, rise to the occasion, and fight back. Here is some advice from someone who knows a lot about war, "Old Blood and Guts" himself, General George S. Patton: "The most vital quality a soldier can possess is self-confidence, utter, complete and bumptious." When you feel that you are in a war with your studies, you will need the same kind of self-confidence.

If you have done everything you can to improve yourself as a student, you should expect miracles but not perfection. You will undoubtedly experience some disappointments even though you are following my system to the letter, but I am certain that you will see amazing progress right from the outset. If you follow my system carefully, you will prevail in the long run because you are on the right track. Moreover, you will find the learning experience to be more enjoyable. It is a natural human tendency to enjoy something when one is good at it. My system will enable you to excel and you will gain enjoyment from constantly scoring high on exams.

What can you expect for all of your efforts? La Rochefoucauld, the French writer, said, "Most people judge men only by their success or their good fortune." Research has shown that persons who make high grades in school are more likely to be successful in other areas. While in school, they are more likely to have friends, participate in extra-curricular activities, and hold school offices. They are also more likely to be successful after graduation. They tend to be more successful in their jobs, if salary and personal recognition are any indication.

More broadly speaking, your studies will influence every aspect of your life. Cicero summed it up over 2,000 years ago, when he said, "These studies are a spur to the young, a delight to the old; an ornament in prosperity, a consoling refuge in adversity; they are a pleasure for us at home, and no burden abroad; they stay up with us at night, they accompany us when we travel, they are with us in our country visits."

You know what your mission is—to become a straight-A student. If I had known the principles presented in this book when I started college as an undergraduate, I would have reached this goal much sooner. Now that you have read this book, you do not have the same excuse. Follow the advice given in *The Epistle of Paul the Apostle to the Philippians*, "This one thing I do, forgetting those things which are behind, and reaching forth unto those things which are before, I press toward the mark."

I will leave you with one final thought from Robert Louis Stevenson, which described what life is all about:

PRINCIPLE 2
"To be what we are, and to become what we are capable of becoming, is the only end of life."

SUMMARY

PART FOUR
MAKING THE SYSTEM WORK FOR YOU

PRINCIPLE 1
Develop the proper study habits and practice them continually if you want to become a straight-A student.

PRINCIPLE 2
"To be what we are, and to become what we are capable of becoming, is the only end of life."
—Robert Louis Stevenson

REFERENCES

Adler, Mortimer J. and Van Doren, Charles. *How to Read a Book*, Simon and Schuster, New York, 1972.

Apps, Jerold W. *Study Skills for Adults Returning to School*, McGraw-Hill Book Company, New York, 1982.

Amstrong, William H. and Lampe, M. Willard II. *Study Tips*, Barron's Educational Series, Inc., New York, 1983.

Bartlett, John. *Familiar Quotations*, Fourteenth Edition, Little, Brown and Company, Boston, Massachusetts, 1968.

Carnegie, Dale. *How to Win Friends & Influence People*, Revised edition, Simon and Schuster, New York, 1981.

Dewey, John. *How We Think*, Heath, Boston, Massachusetts, 1933.

Feder, Bernard, *The Complete Guide to Taking Tests*, Prentice-Hall, Inc., Englewood Cliffs, New Jersey, 1979.

Grassick, Patrick. *Making the Grade*, Arco Publishing, Inc., New York, 1983.

Robinson, Francis P. *Effective Study*, Harper & Bros., New York, 1946

Staton, Thomas F. *How to Study*, McQuiddy Printing Co., Nashville, Tennessee, 1954.

The Home Book of Quotations, Ninth Edition, Burton Stevenson, ed., Dodd, Mead, & Company, New York, 1958.

The Oxford Dictionary of Quotations, Third Edition, Oxford University Press, Oxford, England, 1979.

Turabian, Kate L. *Student's Guide for Writing College Papers*, 3rd edition, The University of Chicago Press, Chicago, Ill., 1976

Voeks, Virginia. *On Becoming an Educated Person*, W.B. Saunders Company, Philadelphia, Pennsylvania, 1964.

APPENDIX
KEY WORDS USED IN
EXAMINATIONS*

KEY TERMS OF QUANTITY, DURATION, OR DEGREE

All, always	Necessarily	—any exception makes
Only	Necessary	these statements
Without exception	Never	false
	No, None	
Rarely	Almost always,	—imply a judgment of
Seldom, Infrequent(ly)	Usual(ly), Often,	frequency or
Occasional(ly)	Frequent(ly)	probability
Some, Sometimes	Probably	
Few	Many	
Several	Most	
About, Around	Approximate(ly)	

DESCRIPTIVE AND ANALYSIS QUESTIONS

Describe, Review —give account of the attributes of the subject under discussion (inherent characteristics, qualities)

*As printed in Grassick, *Making the Grade*, Arco Publishing, Inc., New York, 1983. This material was orginally adapted from Jason Millman and Walter Pauk, *How to Take Tests*, McGraw-Hill, New York, 1969.

Discuss	—tell all you know about the subject that is relevant to the questions under consideration
State	—briefly "describe" with minimal elaboration
Analyze	—separate the subject into parts and examine the elements of which it is composed
Enumerate, List, Tabulate	—briefly present the sequence of elements constituting the whole
Develop	—from a given starting-point, evolve a logical pattern leading to a valid conclusion
Trace	—in narrative form, describe the progress, development, or historical events related to a specific topic from some point of time to a stated conclusion.
Outline, Summarize	—give the theme and main points of the subject in concise form.
Diagram, Sketch	—outline the principle *distinguishing* features of an object or process using a clearly labelled diagram

EXPLANATION AND PROOF QUESTIONS

Explain, Interpret	—state the subject in simpler, more explicit terms
Define, Formulate	—classify the subject; specify its unique qualities and characteristics
Prove, Justify, Show that	—demonstrate validity by test, argument, or evidence
Demonstrate	—explain or prove by use of significant examples
Illustrate	—explain fully by means of diagrams, charts, or concrete examples

COMPARISON QUESTIONS

Compare	—investigate and state the likeness or similarities of two or more subjects
Contrast	—look for noticeable differences

| Relate | —establish the connection between one or more things |

PERSONAL JUDGMENT QUESTIONS

Criticize, Evaluate	—judge or evaluate the subject for its truth, beauty, worth, or significance; and justify your evaluation. "Criticize" doesn't necessarily mean a hostile attack—it is more a matter of comment on literal or implied meaning.
Interpret	—explain and evaluate in terms of your own knowledge
Justify	—ordinarily this implies that you justify a statement on the author's terms. When asked to justify your own statements, defend your position in detail and be convincing.

PROBLEM/SOLUTION QUESTIONS

| Find
Solve
Calculate
Determine
Derive
What is . . . ? | —using the data provided (some of which may be irrelevant) apply mathematical procedures and the principles of formal logical analysis to find a specific quantity in specific units. |

NOTES

NOTES

NOTES

NOTES

NOTES

NOTES

NOTES

NOTES

NOTES

ABOUT THE AUTHOR

Gordon W. Green, Jr. is well qualified to write this book. He received an A in every graduate course he took in route to receiving a Ph.D in economics from The George Washington University in February 1984. This accomplishment was quite remarkable, considering that Dr. Green was attending graduate school part-time in the evening, working more than full-time at his regular job, and taking care of home and family responsibilities at the same time. Even with this busy schedule, he had plenty of time for leisure activities. Dr. Green attributes his success to a unique system of study that he developed, which is the subject of this book.

Dr. Green also is Assistant Chief of the Population Division at the Bureau of the Census, where he directs the preparation of the Nation's statistics on income distribution and poverty. His Ph.D. dissertation received national attention, including a front-page article in *The New York Times*, articles in several other newspapers and magazines, and an appearance on national television to discuss his findings. His work is widely published in government periodicals, magazines, and professional journals. Dr. Green lives with his wife, Maureen, and three children in Fairfax, Virginia.